RULE OF
72

Tom Jacobs
John Del Vecchio

Delray Publishing
55 NE 5th Avenue, Suite 200
Delray Beach FL, 33483
1-888-211-2215
www.dentresearch.com

ISBN: 978-0-692-72135-3

ABOUT THE AUTHORS

Tom Jacobs

Co-Author of *What's Behind The Numbers: A Guide To Exposing Financial Chicanery And Avoiding Huge Losses In Your Portfolio*, Tom bought his first stock at age 12 and started his first business at 15. Influenced by his Depression-era parents to reduce risk and avoid hype, he employs the value strategies in this book to manage individual accounts for clients of all ages and means. Tom is an Investment Advisor and Portfolio Manager with Huckleberry Capital Management, www.investhuckleberry.com. He holds degrees from the University of Chicago Law School and Cornell University and lives with his husband in Marfa, Texas.

✉ *tom@tomjacobs.net*
🐦 *@tomjacobsinvest*
f *tomjacobsinvests*
in *www.linkedin.com/in/tomjacobsinvests*

John Del Vecchio

Co-Author of *What's Behind The Numbers: A Guide To Exposing Financial Chicanery And Avoiding Huge Losses In Your Portfolio*, John is a forensic accountant at heart. Standing on the shoulders of the great David Tice, James O'Shaughnessy and Dr. Howard Schilit, he built a framework of algorithms and a multi-factor grading system that has made him one of the more successful short-sellers around. John graduated summa cum laude from Bryant College with a B.S. in Finance and was awarded Beta Gamma Sigma honors. He earned the right to use the Chartered Financial Analyst designation in September 2001.

 jd@pbxresearch.com
🐦 *@delvecchiojd*

CONTENTS

Why It's All About the Benjamin(s)

Most of us want not only to do *well*, but also do *good*. There is no better example than this man:

Ben Franklin's will included an unusual gift—1,000 pounds sterling each to the cities of Boston and Philadelphia. That's equivalent to about $122,000 today—good money, but hardly riches. The bequests came with strings. For the first 100 years, the money could only be used to loan to help young tradesmen starting out—just as others had loaned money to him. Franklin chose to invest his estate in the future of America, apprentices who would grow businesses and form the backbone of his favored cities. The interest paid on the loans would grow the entire amount over time.

At 100 years, the cities could withdraw 75% of the money to use for "public works, which may be judged of most general utility to the inhabitants, such as fortifications, bridges, aqueducts, public buildings, baths, pavements, or whatever may make living in the town more convenient to its people, and render it more agreeable to strangers resorting thither for health or a tem-porary residence," as well as water systems to bring water to and reduce water waste in Philadelphia. In another 100 years, all the money would go to the cities. Here is what this great believer in compound interest willed:

I have considered that, among artisans, good apprentices are most likely to make good citizens, and, having myself been bred to a manual art, printing, in my native town, and afterwards assisted to set up my business in Philadelphia by kind loans of money from two friends there, which was the foundation of my fortune, and all the utility in life that may be ascribed to me, I wish to be useful even after my death, if possible, in forming and advancing other young men, that may be serviceable to their country in both these towns. To this end, I devote two thousand pounds sterling, of which I give one thousand thereof to the inhabitants of the town of Boston, in Massachusetts, and the other thousand to the inhabitants of the city of Philadelphia, in trust, to and for the uses, intents, and purposes herein after mentioned and declared . . .

The said sum[s are to be loaned out] at five per cent, per annum, to such young married artificers, under the age of twenty-five years, as have served an apprenticeship in the said town[s] . . .

If this plan is executed, and succeeds as projected without interruption for one hundred years, the sum will then be one hundred and thirty-one thousand pounds . . .

At the end of this second term, if no unfortunate accident has prevented the operation, the sum will be four millions and sixty one thousand pounds sterling . . .

Franklin estimated 5% annual returns on the money loaned out. The actual rate came to 4%. By 1890, that $9,000 ballooned to $500,000, an inflation-adjusted $13 million today. After withdrawing 75%, by 1990 (the second 100-year deadline) the remainder still fattened to $6.5 million—a cool $12 million in today's dollars. Following his method with less money and not needing two centuries, you can be independent, care for those you love, and do a lot of good. You don't have to shoot the moon, score in Vegas, win the lottery, or find the one-in-100 startup that doesn't blow up.

Many great names have provided valuable tips to making money, but it was the self-made man and champion of the United States middle class, Benjamin Franklin, who knew how to preserve and grow money. And over 200 years ago, too.

But you can be like Ben and grow your Benjamins. This book is about how to compound like Franklin and not wait 200 years. All you need is to be willing to use basic arithmetic and manage your emotions. Not only is there the excellent and well-trod path of dividend reinvestment, but also two *more* ways a company can pay us to own its stock. Using all three—a trifecta—you will grow financial armor to protect your money from self-interested company management and the financial services industry that is most often out to get us. And, we believe, bring you bushels of Benjamins.

To help you successfully plan for, prepare for, and navigate the future, you will learn how to:

1. Use the quick and easy Rule of 72 to help make better money decisions.

2. Use opportunity cost—a way you think already without giving it a name—to better decide where to put your money.

3. Rip up the calendar and change the way you think about your money over time.

4. Understand what you are *really* making, considering inflation, not just the number on your statement.

5. Understand absolute and relative investing returns, and that you can have one or the other, but not both.

6. Rethink risk so you know what you are in for.

7. Conquer the tricks the mind plays to steer you toward poor decisions.

8. Be skeptical of a company's sales, earnings and cash until shown otherwise. Save trust for friends and love.

9. Use three powerful ways to tell whether a company deserves your trust (and money).

10. Above all, be patient. Don't rush. Question authority. Be very wary of people bearing advice. Even us!

As Benjamin Franklin said, "A penny saved is a penny earned." Today more than ever, we need pennies to become Benjamins.

CHECK YOUR KNOWLEDGE

Before we dive into the chapters of this book, we want to highlight some of the common myths about investing and replace them with facts. By checking your own knowledge, you will then more effectively understand the importance of what we want you to take away from reading this book. Follow these 10 commonly held beliefs throughout the book to learn which are fact and which are fiction—and why.

For each question below, circle one: **ALWAYS SOMETIMES NEVER**

1. It's better to wait to invest until you have more life experience and have a higher income

    ALWAYS   **SOMETIMES**   **NEVER**

2. Your percentage of bonds should be your age and the rest your percentage of stocks; e.g., at age 70, you should have 70% in bonds and 30% in stocks.

    ALWAYS   **SOMETIMES**   **NEVER**

3. Over time, you may obtain excellent investment returns without a lot of volatility.

    ALWAYS   **SOMETIMES**   **NEVER**

4. Stock market indexes like the S&P 500 and Wilshire 5000 show the performance of the average stock in the index.

    ALWAYS   **SOMETIMES**   **NEVER**

5. When choosing among the mutual funds your company offers in your 401(k) or other plan, it's smart to choose the funds that did best last year and sell those that performed poorly.

    ALWAYS   **SOMETIMES**   **NEVER**

6. There are many perfectly legal ways company management can make results look better than they really are.

    ALWAYS   **SOMETIMES**   **NEVER**

7. If a company is really good, it doesn't matter what you pay for its stock.

    ALWAYS   **SOMETIMES**   **NEVER**

8. A lower dividend can be better than a higher one if the company is less likely to cut it.

    ALWAYS   **SOMETIMES**   **NEVER**

9. When a company buys back its own stock, it's not creating jobs. It's a waste of money and not good for the economy.

    ALWAYS   **SOMETIMES**   **NEVER**

10. If you are paying your advisor more than 1% of your account value each year, it's probably time to find another advisor.

    ALWAYS   **SOMETIMES**   **NEVER**

CHAPTER 1

Wet Snow and a Long Hill—Rule of 72

Life is like a snowball. The important thing is finding wet snow and a long hill.
—WARREN BUFFETT

THE GOLDEN RULE OF 72

Compound interest is the eighth wonder of the world. He who understands it, earns it . . . he who doesn't . . . pays it.
—*Attributed to* **ALBERT EINSTEIN** *and many, many others*

In 1956, 26-year-old not-yet investing legend Warren Buffett returned to hometown Omaha from New York to start an investment fund. He went door to door, calling on his father's friends. Seeing his threadbare suit and shirt frayed at the cuffs, prospects despaired. But they had seen Warren grow up so they listened politely to their friend's son. Buffett began by explaining the Rule of 72.

He didn't deploy arcane financial jargon, boast of his New York experience, or regale with promises of wealth. Instead, he started with a math concept requiring only simple division. And those who listened and invested became the now-famous Omaha Buffett millionaires.

What was his message? That in order to grow wealth (and avoid crushing debt), the Rule of 72 is all you need to know.

Here's how it works.

> *To grow wealth (and avoid crushing debt), the Rule of 72 is all you need to know.*

Suppose you hand someone $1,000 and ask how long it will take to double (to make another $1,000 to turn it into $2,000), investing it at a 10% annual interest rate (nice if you can get it!). Most people quickly answer "ten years," assuming that 10 years at 10% is 100%, or twice your money.

Not so. *It's not 10 years, but 7.2 years.* How? Because you earn interest on the interest, too—hence "compound" interest! Here is how interest-on-interest works, using 10% to get to doubling money in 7.2 years:

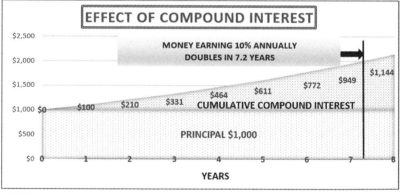

FIGURE 1.1

So for another example, at 5% per year your money doubles in 14.4 years, not 20. Divide 72 by an interest rate to know how many years it takes money to double at that rate. Or, divide 72 by the number of years in which you want to double money to learn what interest rate you will need. At 9%, your $1,000 doubles in 8 years (72 divided by 9). To double money in 12 years, a 6% annual interest rate is required (72 divided by 12).

Did you know...
To double your money:

1. Divide 72 by your annual interest rate to learn the number of years it takes to double. (72/9% = 8 years to double).
2. Divide 72 by in how many years you want your money to double, to find out the required annual interest rate. (72/12 years = 6% annual interest rate required).

It only gets better. The $2,000 takes another 7.2 years to double, but the original $1,000 triples to $3,000 during the 12th year, $4,000 in the 15th, $5,000 in the 17th and keeps on accelerating. Your money is wet snow rolling down a hill. The longer the hill, the larger the snowball, the more your money grows. See how much steeper the compound interest slope becomes over time:

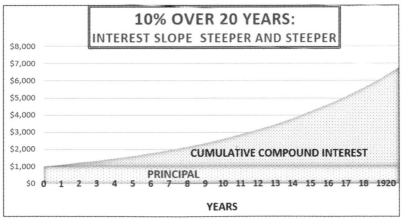

FIGURE 1.2

However, it's not always roses. Remember not only that Albert Einstein said about compound interest: "He who understands it, *earns* it," but also, "He who doesn't, *pays* it." Say we charge a $100 coat on a 12% interest credit card. If we never make a payment, our debt doubles in six years. In the real world a minimum payment is required, but interest eats up most of it. The point remains: Compounding rewards the saver but shackles the debtor.

> ### Do you know...
> How many doubling periods you have in your life? Refer to www.ruleof72book.com to find a calculator that will give you your answer!

So *don't wait* to pay off your high interest debt and find a dollar, wet snow, and a hill. Have as many doubling periods as possible. It's never too early or late. Begin your journey to financial independence *now*.

BE REAL: DON'T FORGET INFLATION

By a continuing process of inflation, government can confiscate, secretly and unobserved, an important part of the wealth of their citizens.

> ——**JOHN MAYNARD KEYNES,** *Economist, Author, and Speculator*

Inflation is taxation without legislation.

> ——**MILTON FRIEDMAN,** *Nobel Laureate in Economics*

The Rule of 72 tells us that even low inflation rates can put a serious dent in your savings and investments over time. For instance, if you bought something that cost a dollar at the creation of the Federal Reserve in December 1913—our third, not first, central bank system—inflation means that it would cost you $23.61 today. Or, if you had left that dollar bill under the mattress and your descendants found it today, it would buy a mere four cents or 4% of what it snared back then. Yes, that may be 103 years, but you get the idea.

> **Did you know...**
> The U.S. Bureau of Labor Statistics has a CPI (consumer price index) Inflation Calculator on their website, showing the change in cost of a basket of goods from one period to another. It's far from perfect, but it's helpful to know the trends. http://www.bls.gov/data/inflation_calculator.htm

Inflation renders plain old (nominal) numbers meaningless over time. A millionaire in 1913 really had some wealth. To have the same purchasing power today, Richie Rich would need $24,000,000. (A dollar in 1913 has a mere 4.166 *cents* worth of purchasing power today.) A millionaire then is a millionaire now, but only in actual numbers, which we call the "nominal" amount. The number that takes inflation into account is the "real" inflation-adjusted number.

Many people learned this the hard way. In the high inflation early 1980s, it was possible to earn 10% annual interest in a money market account! It seemed too good to be true, and it was. Inflation was as high as 18%, so the "amazing" nominal 10% increase was a real 8% decrease! Oops.

So why have inflation at all?

The Federal Reserve prefers inflation (an increase in prices and fall in value of money) to deflation (falling prices)—because *widespread* deflation is horrific. (Note that isolated deflation, as we've seen with computers and other consumer electronics, can be very good.) If your dollar buys more tomorrow

> Inflation is a stealth "tax." The government doesn't collect it from us directly. It does so indirectly, because the Federal Reserve's low inflation target eats away at our money. Stealthy indeed, but it beats deflation!

than today, why spend it? Money and the economy stop dead, and people lose jobs and have nothing to spend, no matter how low prices fall. Investing writer Mark Hulbert calculated that the stock market returned to its pre-Crash of 1929 high within six years because of deflation, not the oft-repeated date of 1954. Hulbert uses the real number, while those who cite 1954 use the nominal number. Nevertheless, few benefitted from deflation's effect on the stock market, because most everyone had to sell stocks and couldn't buy because deflation killed jobs and spending.

This is why the Federal Reserve tries to tweak monetary policy to maintain inflation in the system, but only enough so no one really complains. If it's small, they think, no one will notice that it's a stealth tax.

Note that the "tax" isn't the same for everyone. No single inflation number fits all. In fact, inflation and deflation are realities we have to deal with in terms of costs and income, as presented in this comic. What may be a rising cost for one person isn't for another. Sally, who

grows all her own food from seed, won't experience the same inflation bite as her friend Steve, who pays rising vegetable and fruit prices at the grocery store which, in turn, must pay rising wages. Also, low inflation doesn't impact a wealthier person as much as another who is just getting by.

Nor is it always bad. Inflation *helps* borrowers at fixed rates. If your mortgage is a fixed 4% and inflation is 4%, your *real* interest rate is 0%. Free money! Not so good for the lender, who earns the same *nominal* interest rate but less *real* money if rates rise. This is why in today's low-inflation environment not all banks offer 30-year fixed rate mortgages; they want to be able to lend at higher rates later. That's also why many prefer to offer floating rates that would rise with inflation.

> **Did you know...**
> A return to a gold standard—where all printed money must be backed by the equivalent in gold—is no cure-all for inflation. The U.S. experienced plenty of inflation under the gold standard. Plus, the government, as it did under Franklin Roosevelt, may devalue the gold-paper money exchange rate with inflationary consequences.

No one knows what lies ahead, but you are ready. Whether we face deflation or inflation, you will know the real, not nominal, progress of your money over time. The purpose of all investing is at minimum to protect ourselves from inflation. The rest is gravy.

YOUNG PEOPLE: THEIR GREATEST OPPORTUNITY AND GREATEST IMPEDIMENT

Time is your friend, impulse is your enemy.
            —*Investing Legend* **JOHN C. BOGLE**, *Founder of The Vanguard Group*

We know that teens take risks—we all did when we were that age!—but what we may not know is *why* they take them. These tendencies can continue even into our thirties. This is an important point not only for parents who may waste too much breath—but also for growing money.

A *New Yorker* article by Elizabeth Kolbert, "The Terrible Teens," presents the two dominant neuroscience theories for why teens embrace risk. Neurologist Frances Jensen asserts that the electric lines from all over the brain to the frontal lobe are not fully developed until our twenties or even thirties. The frontal lobe is the center of planning, self-awareness, and judgment, so if it doesn't receive enough impulses, it can't exercise those functions to override poor decisions. The young aren't heedless; they simply lack proper wiring.

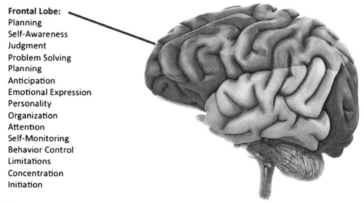

Frontal Lobe:
Planning
Self-Awareness
Judgment
Problem Solving
Planning
Anticipation
Emotional Expression
Personality
Organization
Attention
Self-Monitoring
Behavior Control
Limitations
Concentration
Initiation

FIGURE 1.3

The second is Laurence Steinberg's theory that the pleasure center, the *nucleus accumbens,* grows from childhood to its maximum size in our teens and declines thereafter. Therefore at puberty our dopamine receptors, which signal pleasure, multiply. He says this is why nothing ever feels as good again as when we are teens, whether listening to music, being with friends, or other things not printable in a family book. He maintains that teens are no "worse than their elders at assessing danger. It's just that the potential rewards seem—and from a neurological standpoint, genuinely are—way greater." Teen brains balance risk and reward and choose the greater risk for greater potential reward.

Because the brain encourages spending *now*, when the rewards seem greater, they may miss the key element of growing money: *time.* As mentioned earlier, money is like wet snow rolling down a hill. The longer the hill, the larger the money snowball grows. Ergo, the younger you are, the longer your hill, the more money you will have. In the following table, Saver A who starts investing at 26 never catches up to Saver B who starts at 18 and stops at turning 26—*even though Saver A contributes five times as much money!*

TABLE 1.1 Start Saving Early!

Saver A spends money partying for 8 years, then opens a tax-deferred retirement account earning 12% at age 26 and invests $150/month for the next 40 years				Saver B invests $150/month for 8 years in a tax-deferred account earning 12% and saves NOTHING for the next 40 years	
Which Saver Ends Up with More Money?					
ANNUAL AMOUNT	TOTAL	AGE	ANNUAL AMOUNT	TOTAL	
$0	$0	18	$1,800	$1,902	
$0	$0	19	$1,800	$4,046	
$0	$0	20	$1,800	$6,462	
$0	$0	21	$1,800	$9,183	
$0	$0	22	$1,800	$12,250	
$0	$0	23	$1,800	$15,706	
$0	$0	24	$1,800	$19,600	
$0	$0	25	$1,800	$23,989	
$1,800	$1,902	26	$0	$26,868	
$1,800	$4,046	27	$0	$30,092	
$1,800	$6,462	28	$0	$33,703	
$1,800	$9,183	29	$0	$37,747	
$1,800	$12,250	30	$0	$42,277	
$1,800	$34,506	35	$0	$74,506	
$1,800	$74,937	40	$0	$131,305	
$1,800	$148,386	45	$0	$231,405	
$1,800	$281,827	50	$0	$407,815	
$1,800	$524,245	55	$0	$718,709	
$1,800	$964,644	60	$0	$1,266,610	
$1,800	**$1,764,716**	65	$0	**$2,232,200**	
By age 65, Saver B has *$467,000 more* than Saver A!					

This is an artificial example, of course. There are all sorts of rational reasons for a late start—earning an advanced degree, investing in children, starting a business—but they are ones formed by more developed brains. So because of the obvious benefits of time, we must be creative to counter the money deci-

Americans are saving dramatically less as a percentage of income . . . and younger people are dragging down the average.

sions of higher risk-taking young brains. Especially when Americans are saving dramatically less as a percentage of income . . .

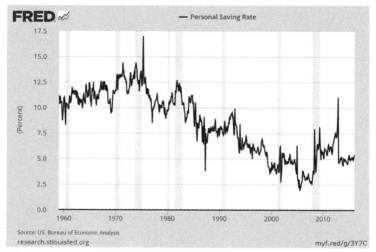

FRED ⚏ — Personal Saving Rate

FIGURE 1.4

. . . and as we'd expect, younger people are dragging down the average:

CHECK YOUR KNOWLEDGE #1

"It's better to wait to invest until you have a higher income."

NEVER. *The earlier you start to save and invest, the better off you will be. See Rule of 72, wet snow and long hill, Saver A and Saver B.*

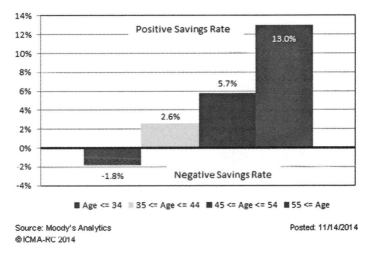

Source: Moody's Analytics
©ICMA-RC 2014

Posted: 11/14/2014

FIGURE 1.5

Here's one way to help. One dad required his son to have an after-school job starting at 15, which eliminated clubs and sports. However, he told his son that so long as he saved $2,000 (a lot then) for college, the rest was his to spend. That turned resentment at lost after-school activities into the satisfaction of a full wallet. The incentive not only produced spending money but also forced better time management. Change "college" to any number of savings goals (vacation, car, house), and presto, you have an incentive plan.

Brain science tells us young people take risks because they can't help it and therefore may potentially miss the irreplaceable benefits of saving and investing earlier and younger. Applying a win-win approach like that of this wily dad can work wonders. But don't despair if you are more like Saver A. As you read this book, you will learn how you can make up some of those years by properly investing now and ahead.

FOMO AND THE $15 MILLION DECK: OPPORTUNITY COST

Intelligent people make decisions based on opportunity cost.

——**CHARLIE MUNGER,** *Vice-Chairman of Berkshire Hathaway*

"Fear of missing out," or FOMO, is today's disease of those who have everything available with a text or app. Actor/comedian Aziz Ansari nails this condition of urban singles in his live shows. The theme: When everything is available, what do you choose? FOMO is another way to explain opportunity cost.

In one of his stand-up routines, an Ansari character is tormented at lunchtime. What if by going to *this* taco stand he misses out on the *best* taco at another? Or, he wants a date for a concert and asks woman number two after finding his first choice is busy. But then number one suddenly is available. Is he a jerk if he cancels number two in favor of number one? Of course he is! But the fear of missing out torments him. *"What if she is The One?"* he worries, so he makes the jerk move. She proves to be a nightmare.

Our money faces the same option. Every day we decide where to put it. Do we pay to eat out or pack a lunch? Do we buy a used car or a new one? Should we invest in further education or head out into the world to make our fortunes? Take time off and travel the world? Each choice not only has a *visible* price tag, but also an *invisible* one—an *opportunity cost.*

In 2015, American consumers for the first time spent more on dining out than in the grocery store. We are busier than ever and for the 1992–2015 period, dining out became not only more convenient but also a necessity for many people.

The roughly $10 billion 1992 gap between the grocery store and dining out narrowed to zero in two decades. But that's a narrowing gap *each year.* Therefore, American consumers have diverted *tens of billions* from their pockets to restaurant and bar owners.

Assuming that eating at home is cheaper than dining out—think of the cost of drinks, for one thing—what could consumers have done with even part of that money saved? What would investing it have gained? That's the opportunity cost. This is one reason that Buffett as a child could barely bring himself to spend money earned from his paper route. His math skills told him the significant opportunity cost because he knew how much it could compound if not spent.

If you put the money *here*, not *there*, what will your result be, especially when there is no way of knowing for sure? Yet we *must* have a view about the future or we wouldn't get up in the morning. We can't have Aziz's paralysis. We must take the information we have, estimate, and act.

> Opportunity Cost: If you put the money *here*, not *there*, what will your result be, especially when there is no way of knowing for sure?

Some prefer better odds and less risk while others want the opposite: to gamble with very poor odds, great risk, and the remote chance of the Big Score. Wait for the light or dash across the street? Get in a car, plane, or space mobile? Take a chance on a new job or stick with the devil you know? We calculate odds all day long, whether we know it or not. Each decision is all about opportunity cost.

True story. A man in Omaha wanted to put a deck on his house, a place for family and friends to gather and have fun. A sturdy Midwesterner, his deck would be equally sturdy. It was the deck to end all decks, built to last. He paid a lot for it but imagined the good times ahead.

Yet this deck cost him $15 million without his even knowing it.

He financed the deck by selling some of his stock in Berkshire Hathaway, the Warren Buffett-led company. As one of the original Buffett investors in the 1950s, he had plenty of Berkshares, so decided he wouldn't miss a few.

After years of enjoying the barbecues and community on the deck, his friends did a little math. It seems that after selling the stock to finance the deck, Berkshire continued to go up, up, *ballooning 32 times*—$10,000 became $320,000—in less than a decade. They calculated that the stock their friend sold, with inflation, would have been worth $15 million. That's some big opportunity cost!

Let's sum it up with this illustration:

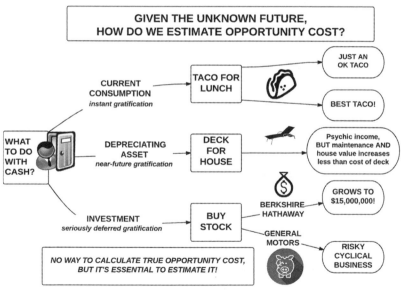

FIGURE 1.6

What do we give up when we make a choice? We don't know, but we have to consider it. Whether it's as minor as choosing the second-best taco, or as life changing as building a $15 million deck, FOMO is opportunity cost in action:

FIGURE 1.7 Thanks to Ryan O'Connor, Principal of Fountain Square Capital Management, for the story of Buffett visiting his grandparents, who then became original Buffett Partnership members in the 1950s, and also for this chapter's tale and photo of those grandparents' "$15 million deck."

BAMBI MEETS GODZILLA

Losing some money is an inevitable part of investing, and there's nothing you can do to prevent it. But to be an intelligent investor, you must take responsibility for ensuring that you never lose most or all of your money.

—BENJAMIN GRAHAM

In the two-minute cartoon *Bambi Meets Godzilla,* Bambi frolics gently in the forest to the sound of sweet music. Once we are lulled into the happy scene, a giant foot appears and squashes Bambi.

That's pretty much all we need to know about investing. From the early 1980s to 2000, there was not one single stock market panic. (The crash of 1987 was brief and the market soon raced to new highs.) The market would always go up! Buy on the dips! We were fearless, similar to Bambi joyfully frolicking in the forest, oblivious to the danger ahead.

Then Godzilla came. The 2000–02 and 2008–09 crashes reminded us that markets do have cycles.

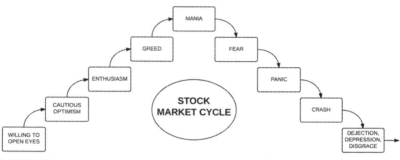

FIGURE 1.8

Investors hadn't seen anything like it since 1973–74, which means almost no one remembered anything bad. Yet actually, the 1982–2000 bull market of the so-called great moderation was an exception, not the rule. Important context comes in the 1893 *A Brief History of Panics in the United States*, by the French doctor and statistician Clément Juglar (1819–1905).

It turns out that in the 1813–1893 period covered by Juglar's book, there was a full-on recession at best and depression at worst every decade or so in the United States: 1814, 1818, 1825–26, 1831, 1837–39, 1848, 1857, 1864, 1873, 1884, and 1888–92. These were followed by 1893–94, 1903, 1907, and 1913. Forgotten today is that the late 1800s depression made the 1930s look like a walk in Central Park. Where, by the way, the newly destitute in and around New York City camped, cooked over fires, and tended what animals they still had.

> **Did you know...**
> While employment goes hand in hand with the economic cycle, it does not with the stock market. The stock market rises before high unemployment and low expectations improve, and it declines before high employment and high expectations worsen.
>
> | Unemployment Rate | S&P 500 Annualized Returns |
> | --- | --- |
> | Above 9% | 24.5% |
> | 7-9% | 15.1% |
> | 5-7% | 8.3% |
> | Below 5% | 3.9% |

Then, miraculously, only four big ones followed: the 1929 Crash and Great Depression, 1973–74, 2000–02, and the 2008–09 Great Recession. Gosh, did the birth of the third Federal Reserve System in 1913 save us from extremes for all time, turning on and off the printing press with the precision of a Swiss watchmaker?

No.

According to one theory of finance, the longer an unstable system remains stable, the worse the eventual consequences. Consider any of the balancing acts, notably those on *Survivor* (all knowledge flows from reality TV). There is calm on the log or tightrope, then the occasional midcourse correction, and finally, if given enough time, the crash and splash. The longer we maintain stability on an inherently unstable log, the worse the fall will be. There is no halfway measure. Eventually you crash and then you die.

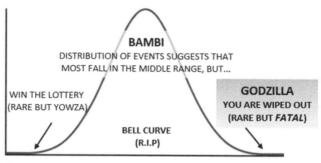

FIGURE 1.9

This is one reason the Bell Curve is of no use in investing. Perhaps most results will fall within a safe range, but if you're Bambi you don't care if everyone else is average. Godzilla events may be rare, but Juglar and Benoit Mandelbrot, among others, show convincingly that they are far more common than the Bell Curve predicts. When Bambi meets Godzilla, Bambi does not invest the next day.

Do we *want* more frequent gut wrenching, community destroying, and life-upending economic and stock market events? No, but they are unavoidable. The longer we go without them, the worse they will be. No one has repealed stock market and economic cycles, which Juglar showed go back to our earliest days. The danger is to forget that these happen, to think that the 38% drop in the S&P 500 market index in 2008 and the Great Recession were rare outliers, when they are the rule. Enjoy the happy days in the forest, but expect the darker days that come. Be prepared. Which, as it happens, the next chapter is all about.

CHAPTER 2

What Is Risk?

Successful investing is about managing risk, not avoiding it.

—BENJAMIN GRAHAM

CONSERVATIVE, MODERATE OR AGGRESSIVE?

The defensive (or passive) investor will place chief emphasis on the avoidance of serious mistakes or losses. His second aim will be freedom from effort, annoyance, and the need for making frequent decisions.

The determining trait of the enterprising (or active, or aggressive) investor is his willingness to devote time and care to the selection of securities that are both sound and more attractive than the average.

—BENJAMIN GRAHAM

Chapter 2 is about risk—not what the financial services industry or most people think it is, but what it *really* is and what to do about it.

A typical conversation with an advisor starts with, "Are you a conservative, moderate, or aggressive investor?" The industry must ask you so it can plug you into cookie cutter investment software programs to reduce risk that should you complain, mediate, or arbitrate, the firm will be protected.

Whether you walk into an advisor's office, crack a beginning investing book, or decipher information from a company's 401(k) plan mutual fund options, the three words are everywhere. They purport to define attitude toward risk so you can determine your investing course of action. Because the industry is driven by marketing so they may collect the most dollars and fees from people, it uses whatever terms work. The three words may work for the industry, but that doesn't mean they are right or work for you.

Standard financial service industry advice is that "conservative," "moderate," and "aggressive" refer to what percentages of your money to have in stocks and bonds. The idea is that bonds are somehow "safer" than stocks so you are more likely to have your money when you need it. Stocks represent more risk but offer greater potential return. This is, like all simple answers to complex questions, wrong.

But what these terms are really getting at is the wrong definition of risk. Most people don't know it but they think risk is *volatility*—how rapid and how much change there is in the value of their investments. How much market fluctuation you can handle and still sleep at night is supposed to be "risk tolerance."

Nothing is "safe." This book aims to help take as much risk—the chance of losing all your money—out of the equation as possible.

And it is true, for the most part, that a greater percentage in bonds will deliver less volatility—less bouncing around—of your account value than a greater percentage in stocks. But bonds may not always be less volatile, and they come with inflation and interest rate risk, as we'll see soon.

Most people believe that and behave as if market drops will wipe out their money (so they sell) and that we should all have an endlessly rising market (so they keep buying expensively). The industry has learned to play on that. It lulls people into a false sense of safety by fine tuning the percentage of stocks and bonds according to which of the magic three types you are—conservative, moderate, or aggressive. It's not wrong to do this. In fact, if you are afraid of volatility, by all means, choose percentages. But as you will see in this chapter, "safety" is a myth, there is no investing without risk, and the real risk is not volatility, but the possibility that you will lose all your money. And because that possibility is always there with stocks or bonds—even some money market funds blew up in the 2008 crash!—nothing is "safe." This book aims to help take as much risk—the chance of losing all your money—out of the equation as possible. This increases the opportunity to make money.

So let's look at the mythical "bond" that allegedly is the high priest of "conservative" investors. There are bonds and then there are bonds. People throw the word "bond" around as if it's one thing and one thing only. No one would make that mistake with stocks. Let's not with bonds. A person's word and company promise to pay may be their bond, but each may break it.

Companies and governments who need money can issue bonds, which are promises to pay interest until an expiration date. At that date, called the bond's maturity, the bond ceases to exist and the issuer repays principal and re maining interest. Bonds come with shorter times to maturity or longer, just as people do. For example, "Tom's Tomatoes" issues bonds paying 4% and maturing in 2025. "Bond Buyer" buys $1,000 worth earning the right to $40 a year in interest payments until maturity in 2025, when the issuer will pay back the $1,000.

> "The investor should be aware that even though safety of its principal and interest may be unquestioned, a long term bond could vary widely in market price in response to changes in interest rates."
> —Benjamin Graham

Once the bonds are sold to investors for the first time, they may buy and sell them on the bond market. They are subject to gain or loss due to interest rate changes and the financial health of the buyer. This chart shows the inverse relationship between bond prices and interest rates:

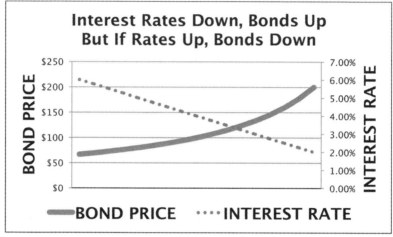

FIGURE 2.1

If a bond at issuance pays 4% annually, and interest rates fall (dotted line and right axis), the bond price rises (solid line, left axis). If rates fall to 2%, the bond should double to $200. Nice, right? But when rates rise, bond prices fall. If they jump to 6%, the bond drops 33% to $67. If the issuer's financial health worsens, investors may fear possible default on the interest and principal payments. Sellers will outnumber buyers, and the bond price will decline until $40 is a high enough percentage rate to balance buyers and sellers. An existing owner who must sell takes a loss.

Yet despite these two risks, bonds hold two distinct advantages over stocks.

First, if a company enters bankruptcy, bondholders are paid before anyone else—maybe not much, but more than the stockholders, who are almost always wiped out. Second, *municipal* issuers, as opposed to *corporations*, very rarely default. Even in the Great Depression, only one state—Arkansas—defaulted on its general obligation bonds, and it was the first state to default since before the Civil War. However, corporate bonds didn't do so well. And so bonds are not "safe" or "riskless," either.

The late Barton Biggs's *Wealth, War and Wisdom* asked if any investment at the start of the 20th century would still be there—worldwide and in any economic conditions—at the end of the century. In searching for what is called a permanent "store of value," he found not gold, real estate, stocks, bonds or Pez dispensers, but only land with water and animals. The catch? Your neighbors will always have more guns to take your resources away from you!

There is no completely safe place for our money. Stocks and bonds, like crossing the street or choosing a spouse, both require analysis of risk and reward with imperfect information. The longer the investing runway, the better the odds for wisely chosen stocks—provided they are chosen with an eye to withstanding Godzilla *and* that you can handle volatility, because the longer time you have, the more likely you will experience extreme bull and bear markets. With bonds, the shorter the time (especially what investors call "duration"—how long until the bond matures, or pays back the bondholders the full face value of the bond), bonds can behave well for us. The longer the duration, the more inflation and price risk.

Risk is not your percentage in bonds or stocks and it's not volatility. Volatility is inescapable if you invest in stocks—even in bonds. It's like potholes in the road. They will always be there. So what are risk and risk tolerance? It's your ability to sleep at night, knowing that there is always risk of losing the entire value of an investment, but also that there are ways to take as much risk as possible out of the equation.

THE GLIDE PATH: A CONTRARIAN VIEW OF THE BOND-STOCK-AGE EQUATION

The time that people need to be most conservative is not in retirement but at the beginning of retirement.

—**LUKE DELORME,** *American Institute for Economic Research*

Now that we have a handle on the myth that risk tolerance dictates your percentage of stocks and bonds, let's attack the idea that age determines that percentage allocation too. The conventional wisdom is that your percentage of bonds should equal your age, with the rest in stocks to equal 100%. For example, if you are 50, your money would be invested 50% in stocks and 50% in bonds, and at 80, 20% in stocks and 80% in bonds. The bond percentage increases with age and the stock percentage decreases. Companies offer target-date retirement mutual funds for you based on your expected time to retirement, sparing you the need to watch the percentages and make the changes yourself.

Research, however, is questioning this view and moving to a "glide path," where your percentage of stocks should *increase*, not decrease, with age *after retirement*, and bonds should *decrease*. And you should approach and start retirement with a higher percentage of bonds than the age rule tells us.

There are three reasons for this revolutionary thinking.

First, we live much longer today and need our money for more time after we are not working. Second, if money must last longer, even a little inflation erodes the purchasing power of retirement funds much more than before. And third, the closer you are to retirement, the greater the risk a market drop presents, because you start retirement with less money to draw from.

> **Did you know...**
> The Congressional Budget Office (CBO) reported that in the 15 months up to Oct. 2008, the value of retirement accounts declined by about $2 trillion.

American Institute for Economic Research's Luke Delorme takes a different view. He says we should start retirement at 65 with 80%—not 65%—in bonds, and gradually decrease that to 30% over 30 years to age 95 (we all hope to make it there with both sound mind and body!). Thus stocks would be only 20%, not 35%, at retirement, and *rise gradually to 70% rather than decrease to a tiny 5%* at 95—a *huge* difference.

This is how the conventional wisdom looks versus the glide path as presented by Delorme:

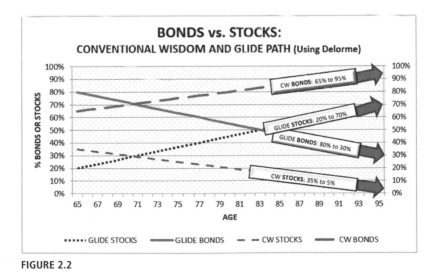

FIGURE 2.2

There is a possible middle way that doesn't involve changing percentages regularly. It offers the stock market potential for inflation protection, dividend income and reinvestment, and also bonds' relative stability but with the opportunity for appreciation on those bonds. It is likely to reduce the risk of a dramatic kick to your retirement assets at the wrong time and give you exposure to the stock market while you are retired. Here's how.

First, choose real estate investment trusts (REITs) with sustainable dividends, manageable debt, and desirable and high-occupancy buildings. This combines shareholder yield with inflation protection, because the leases typically contain provisions for rents to increase with inflation. That means dividends may increase too, maintaining or increasing their real yields (for "real" versus "nominal," see Chapter 1).

Second, own bonds through higher yielding and lower expense closed-end bond funds (CEFs) selling for less than net asset value (NAV). If the value of the fund's bonds is $10 per share, NAV is $10. But if shares sell for $8, there is a built-in 20% potential gain in addition to the dividend yield.

There is no magic formula because each person's situation is different. While the actuarial tables may tell us something, they do not tell us what quality of life we will have or account for different standards of living. Having a pension changes the equation too. And some people are fortunate enough to have money to live on, as well as more they can invest apart from it.

No matter, there's no doubt that the old saw—that your percentage of bonds equals your age—has cut its last log.

> *The old saw—that your percentage of bonds equals your age— has cut its last log.*

CHECK YOUR KNOWLEDGE #2

"Your percentage of bonds should be your age and the rest your percentage of stocks; e.g., at age 70, you should have 70% in bonds and 30% in stocks."

(PROBABLY) NEVER. *The "Glide Path" research supports being overweighted in bonds as you approach retirement, and then gradually increasing stocks after retirement.*

TIME WOUNDS ALL HEELS

. . . long run is a misleading guide to current affairs. In the long run we are all dead. Economists set themselves too easy, too useless a task, if in tempestuous seasons they can only tell us, that when the storm is long past, the ocean is flat again.
——**JOHN MAYNARD KEYNES,** *A Tract on Monetary Reform*

We've seen how Glide Path research turns conventional wisdom about stock and bond allocations upside down. Now, let's attack a related piece of conventional wisdom: the younger you are, the more aggressive an investor you can be—the more money in stocks than bonds—because time heals all wounds. The older you are, the more conservative—more money in bonds than stocks—you should be because you have less time. If you agree with these statements, you are like most people. They believe that *time reduces risk*, which is why we're all taught to think "long-term" about the portion of our retirement savings invested in stocks. Given enough time, everything will "even out." This treats time as a method of diversification.

This view is so widely accepted that to question it is heresy. Yet Northwestern University's John Norstand disagrees, persuasively asserting that time *increases*, not *decreases* risk of loss.

When we invest money, we take the available information and make a decision about the unknown future. We imagine that many things may happen to that money down the road. Think of the range of possible outcomes as light entering and exiting the prism on the cover of Pink Floyd's *Dark Side of the Moon*. A single ray of light shoots into the prism and disperses on the other side into an ever-widening range of many colors (assume the colors). Now consider it in terms of the range of possibilities:

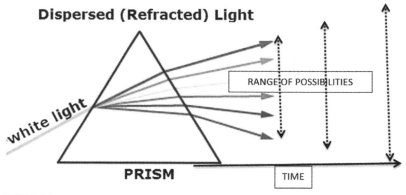

FIGURE 2.3

The more time, the greater the range of possible outcomes. (If you are a scientist or statistician, please be kind.) This is greater, not lesser, risk over time. The longer we invest, the *more* likely the extreme event that wipes out substantial wealth.

> *The longer we invest, the more likely the extreme event that wipes out substantial wealth.*

Consider the 1907 panic, 1929 crash and Great Depression, and the 1973–74, 2000–02, and 2008–09 crashes. Intervening periods seemed just fine. From 1920 to 1929, all was good, and then it wasn't. From World War II until 1973, it was mostly smooth sailing. From 1982 to 2000, and 2003 to 2008, the bulls stampeded. And while it may appear that life was dandy from 1968 to 1982, not so. The Dow was flat nominally but inflation delivered a real return of minus 50%. So with enough time, the risk of extreme events *increases*, not decreases. Time is *not* diversification.

We know we can't pick the highs and lows with any consistency, if at all, so we do the best we can with a mix of investments, industries, and management that pays us to own their stock (as you will see in Chapter 5). These help but do not eliminate risk of drawdowns— dramatic drops from peak to trough—but they help. In investing, time does not heal all wounds, but rather (*see*, the Achilles myth) wounds all heels. The Godzilla moment is *more* likely over time, not *less*. Being long-term means being able to expect and prepare for that eventuality according to your risk tolerance.

A CHECKING ACCOUNT THAT PAYS 12%

If it seems too good to be true, it probably is.
——WARREN BUFFETT *(and everyone's dad)*

So far, so good with bonds and risk. Risk tolerance is tolerance of volatility—how much variability you can stomach in your account value. Most people want the potential returns of the stock market with the lower volatility of bonds. This is like having a checking account that pays 12%. Not possible.

Case in point. Once upon a time there was a New York City money manager who earned his clients 12% year in, year out, for decades. His business became huge because of his dependable "secret method." At 12% a year, the Rule of 72 tells us that money doubles every six years. Who wouldn't take that guaranteed return?

The manager was, of course, Bernie Madoff, and his miraculous returns were built on a Ponzi scheme. New client money provided the

12% needed to keep existing clients' profits flowing and him bathing in champagne. But when there weren't enough new clients, it all blew up. His reward was a life sentence, while his family and many clients were ruined.

> ### Did you know...
> Prosecutors estimate Bernie Madoff, head of the largest Ponzi scheme in U.S. history, defrauded investors of $65 *billion*. This dwarfs the famous Charles Ponzi's own scheme, $225 million in 2008 dollars, the year of Madoff's exposure.
>
> **CHARLES PONZI**   **BERNARD MADOFF**
> **SOURCE:** Wikipedia

Among the Madoff lessons, there is one big honking one: *Most people want to make money without risk of losing any, and they'll try just about any way to get it.* Some people will go with allocating between stocks and bonds, but others think they can have it all: stock market returns with bond market volatility.

In investing, that's not possible. Even so-called "safe" government-backed securities and CDs aren't riskless because over time they lose value to inflation. Investors have to put at least some money in the stock market as part of a diversified financial life. And doing so requires understanding risk in order to know how much risk to take.

Stocks that rise and fall are not merely *normal*—they are as *certain* as death and taxes. The stock market is a place where stocks, which are pieces of ownership in businesses, are valued every day by buyers and sellers. Because businesses are not clocks that tick off money on schedule, buyers and sellers change opinions on what various businesses are worth. Their stock prices rise and fall. If you look at a company's stock price that has risen over a long time, you will see many significant ups and downs along the way. Yet in the long run, apart from this short term sound and fury, stocks do well or poorly according to how well businesses produce excess cash and how wisely they spend it. Period.

When a person asks, "I need to make money fast in the stock market. What can you do for me?" the answer should be, "Nothing, except take so much risk of loss that you are likely to lose it all!" There is no such thing as a quick buck, unless they find oil or gold beneath your land or a distant childless relative leaves you a pile. Investing is about growing wealth slowly and accepting the bumps.

There are ways to reduce stock investing risk, such as investing money each month to smooth out your buying prices (see "dollar-cost averaging" in Chapter 3), but the principle remains: If you think there is a checking account—a no risk place for your money—that pays 12% a year, remember Madoff. Otherwise, take the ups and downs in stride. Or to torture a Buddhist teaching: volatility is inevitable, but suffering is optional.

ACT AT LEISURE, REPENT NEVER

In the short run, the market is a voting machine but in the long run, a weighing machine.

—BENJAMIN GRAHAM

In the short term, emotion and popularity rule the market, creating price volatility.

The stock market is an auction. Through humans and computers, markets such as the New York Stock Exchange and the NASDAQ manage buying and selling. They maintain order books, long ago with paper, pencil and pen, but today through constantly changing electronic lists of offers sent by brokerage houses to buy or sell shares of stock in a company. The "bid" is the highest price a buyer will pay at the moment and the "ask" is the lowest at which a seller will sell. When prices match, a trade occurs.

Supply and demand rule the market. If you have more buyers, prices *rise* until the supply of sellers increases to match buyer demand. When there are more sellers, prices *fall* until the supply of buyers matches seller demand.

The shorter the time period, the more stocks rise and fall as buyers and sellers act—*vote*—based on popularity and emotion. In the longer run, buyers and sellers *weigh* the value of this business or that to make considered buying and selling decisions. You can see this at work in any stock's price history. For example, let's take the last five years for Apple, the largest company in the world by market value:

FIGURE 2.4

Even though Apple's five-year direction has been up, there have been significant drops. If you were to stretch this farther side to side, more drops would seem more dramatic in short periods. This works for stocks that slump over time, too. Their prices show short periods in which they jump.

> **Did you know...**
> Steve Jobs returned to Apple in 1997 when it was a few months away from bankruptcy. Apple had a dwindling 4 percent share of the PC market and annual losses exceeding $1 billion. Three CEOs had come and gone in a decade; board members had tried to sell the company but found no takers. Two months after Apple's deal with Microsoft in which Microsoft invested $150 million in the company and agreed to make Office for Mac, Dell CEO Michael Dell told a tech industry symposium that if he ran Apple, he'd "shut it down and give the money back to shareholders." Good thing he wasn't CEO. Apple's $3 billion market cap in 1997 is $550 billion today. —Bloomberg

Who causes the short-term and long-term movements? The first are traders, people or software programs that act compulsively by the day, hour or even second. They care only about price and vote for what's in or what's out at the moment. They are speculators.

> Speculators and traders buy and sell based on popularity, investors by thinking like a business owner.

The other group treats a share of stock as part ownership of a business. Over time, these buyers and sellers weigh the quality and value of a business and make investment decisions carefully. These are investors. They take time to consider such things as management, sales, and cash flow to weigh companies and make better investment decisions.

Emotion and fashion govern prices in the short-term, but thoughtfulness and endurance dominate in the long-run. In investing, to act at leisure is to repent never—or at least more rarely.

DIVIDENDS AS SHOCK ABSORBERS

What, Me Worry?

——*MAD Magazine's* **ALFRED E. NEUMAN** *(probably a dividend investor)*

One of the ways to take some risk out of investing in the stock market is through owning inexpensively-priced dividend-paying stocks. If the dividends are sustainable and you reinvest them, then a declining stock price is both your protector and friend. You sleep at night while others shake. You are Alfred E. Neuman, with better teeth and smaller ears.

Assume you own—but do not throw—"Tom's Tomatoes," a steady but unspectacular (duh, it's got "Tom" in it) tomato grower. You paid an average of $10 a share. Tom's pays $0.50 a year in dividends, so at your $10 purchase price, Tom's dividend yield is 5%.

As always happens, someday the markets turn bearish. The stock crumbles to $8, but the $0.50 dividend remains the same. Buyers at $8 gain a 6.25% yield ($0.50/$8 = 6.25%). If investors truly panic, the price might collapse to $6, but this boosts the yield to 8.33% for new buyers. In today's low inflation environment, these are very, very good yields. Potential buyers lick their lips: "Wow, 8.33%? How often do you get that without risk of a dividend cut?" And many will buy to lock down the juicy yield. With more buyers than sellers, the stock rises. Voilà, the higher yield is a shock absorber and a source of potential profits if the stock returns to former levels:

TABLE 2.1 How Dividend Yield Rises as Stock Price Declines

AS TOM'S TOMATOES STOCK PRICE DROPS . . .	WHILE ITS DIVIDEND REMAINS THE SAME . . .	THE DIVIDEND YIELD RISES . . .	. . . AND ATTRACTS DIVIDEND INVESTORS, PUTTING A FLOOR UNDER TOM'S TOMATOES STOCK PRICE
$10.00	$0.50	5%	
$8.00	$0.50	6.25%	
$6.00	$0.50	8.33%	

Meanwhile, the owner of the non-dividend paying "growth stock" is more likely to panic and sell at exactly the wrong time. That investor has nothing to break the fall.

Fine, but Tom's stock has dropped 20% or 40% in our example. What do we care about another percentage point or two of dividend yield?

So long as you are not selling, you should be sleeping like a (good) baby. The dividend is paid each quarter and you reinvest. The lower shares fall, the more your dividend buys—and at a better yield! You own 100 shares of Tom's. At $10, these bring you $50 a year in dividends, which buy 5 more shares yielding 5%. At $8, the dividends buy 6.25 (when reinvesting dividends, you can buy fractional shares) at a 6.25% yield, and at $6, a lovely 8.33 at 8.33%. As the price drops, you buy more and cheaper shares at a higher yield. This reduces your average cost, sets you up for more profits when the stock's value usually returns to normal, and increases your average yield while you wait. (You'll see this in more detail in Chapter 3.)

"What, me worry?" Indeed!

In a roaring bull market, this strategy seems ho-hum compared to all the market darlings catapulting ever higher. But when investors tire of paying the "price-to-dream ratio" for the stocks, they crash violently. Investors using a value-based dividend reinvestment strategy have shock absorbers and better odds of a brighter future. They sleep soundly.

THE ELEPHANT IN THE BATHTUB

May not the typical large and prosperous company be subject to a two-fold limitation: first, that its very size precludes spectacular growth; second that its high rate of earnings on invested capital makes it vulnerable to attack if not by competition then perhaps by regulation? . . . Perhaps also, the smaller companies and the less popular industries as a class may be definitely undervalued, both absolutely and in relation to the favored issues.

—**BENJAMIN GRAHAM** *and* **DAVID DODD,** *Security Analysis*

Size is the enemy of returns.

—*Yale University Endowment Manager* **DAVID SWENSON**

It's not easy to sell your house and turn it into cash. We say it's not a liquid asset. Cash is the most liquid asset, and the U.S. dollar the most liquid cash. Stock market investors must take that into account when examining their risk tolerance for swings in the value of their stocks and investment accounts.

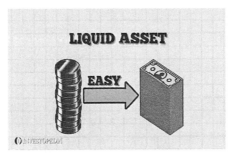

FIGURE 2.5

Larger company stocks trade more shares. They are easier to buy and sell; they have greater liquidity and their prices don't move around a lot. Smaller company stocks have less liquidity so buying and selling can move the price substantially. It can be harder to buy and sell them and in extreme markets very hard at any price. Here's how it works.

It's easy to buy and sell shares of Apple, which trades an average of 53 million shares each day. The bid and ask are usually fractions of pennies apart. You can buy or sell Apple, Google, Amazon, General Electric, Microsoft and other familiar big names in a snap and at good prices because they are very liquid.

> **Did you know...**
> A stock's market value, also called stock market capitalization or "cap," is its number of shares times its stock price.

Apple shares are the elephant in the African river. When a herd of elephants goes for a bath, sure, it's not delicate, but they can all fit. The water ripples and may splash the shores, but that's it. Trading the big stocks is the same.

On the other hand, Tom's Tomatoes is a very small company (for now!), trading a mere 1,000 shares a day. At $10 a share, that's a daily volume of $10,000. Here we have the city elephants, perhaps the Parisians Babar and Celeste, who prefer the convenience and privacy of the bathtub. When they step in, it's a cannonball in a kiddie pool: water explodes everywhere.

Same thing if you want to buy or sell $1,000 worth of Tom's—10% of the daily volume—where for Apple it would be 0.0000000000000000000001% (Didn't actually calculate those zeroes). The order will splash the bid and ask all over the place. It will take a long time to sell that $1,000, and likely not at a favorable price. The buyer or seller has to blink and take less or pay more than desired. Tom's is an illiquid stock.

Your Apple, Microsoft, or Facebook stock will rise or fall more slowly, and because the market indexes are weighted more heavily towards the largest companies, the indexes too won't be very volatile. Owning Tom's Tomatoes stock, conversely, can feel like bungee jumping. This is why  most people prefer the established large company stock's relative stability, but they must also accept lower potential returns. On the other hand, smaller company stocks' greater volatility makes people nervous, but on average smaller companies offer higher expected returns. An investor has to weigh the pros and cons of higher and lower liquidity.

> *Did you know...*
> The S&P 500 is an index of 500 large companies, while the Russell 2000 is an index of the bottom 2,000 of the Russell 3000 index. The S&P 500 tracks large company performance (average market value is $58 *billion*), while the Russell 200 tracks small company (average market value $526 *million*) performance.

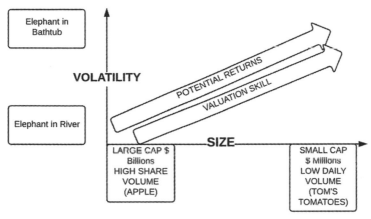

FIGURE 2.6

For example, from September 2015 to early 2016, the Russell 2000 index of smaller companies fell twice as much as the large company index S&P 500, −22% to the S&P's −11% at one point. When things eventually turn, smaller companies *rise* more than the S&P 500.

Anyone can buy liquid stocks of large companies with long histories without too much fear of losing everything. It's also easy to do through index mutual funds that mimic the S&P 500 market index. However, more skills are required to jump into the volatile small company tub. This book—especially the six tests in Chapters 4 and 5—will help increase the chances of excellent profits and decrease the chances of blowups in all stocks, but especially in the smaller ones.

CHECK YOUR KNOWLEDGE #3

"Over time, you may obtain excellent investment returns without a lot of volatility."

NEVER. *Any investment returns require the investor to accept volatility. To achieve very good or excellent returns, an investor must accept more volatility and have greater valuation skill so as to pick smaller company stocks.*

ABSOLUTIST OR RELATIVIST: THE RIGHT TOOL FOR THE JOB

We urge the beginner in security buying not to waste his efforts and his money in trying to beat the market. Let him study security values and initially test out his judgment on price versus value with the smallest possible sums.

—BENJAMIN GRAHAM

It would be nice to have 12% returns year after year without volatility, but that isn't possible. But how to measure our returns? How to know if we are doing well or poorly? It depends on whether you seek absolute or relative returns, and it's nearly impossible to have both over time.

In saving and investing, a relativist is obsessed with "beating the market" or "doing better than the indexes." If a market index such as the S&P 500 were to rise 5%, the relativist wants her account to fatten *at least* 5%. On the other hand, the absolutist cares only that her account grows greater than or equal to the inflation rate regardless of the indexes. The relativist wants *relative* returns and the absolutist wants *absolute* returns. There is no right or wrong, but you can't have both for long because each type of returns requires different volatility.

Volatility is how dramatically market indexes and individual stock prices rise and fall. Think of the water in a bathtub (you already know about the elephant getting in). In the low-volatility absolute returns world, the bathtub water is mostly undisturbed by whatever is going on around it. The index-investing world, ruled by the larger companies in the indexes, is more volatile. Here, an investor is willing to get into the tub even though the water splashes about, because it's the same for everyone who takes a bath.

But to achieve really good relative returns, the investor must do *something different* than buy all the same big companies that everyone else and the indexes own. "Something different" usually requires smaller, unknown companies, whose stocks are very volatile. Their prices slosh out of the bathtub and splash all over the bathroom, just like the elephant clambering into the tub. Relative returns investors must accept greater volatility.

Yet people fight the reality that positive relative returns and absolute returns don't mix. Harvard Law professor Alan Dershowitz says that a conservative is a liberal who just got mugged (and a liberal is a conservative who has just been arrested). Similarly, the absolute returns investor is a relative returns investor who just experienced a large *drawdown*. A drawdown is a normal, inevitable, unavoidable drop in the market indexes, bringing all stocks with it. (As opposed to a *loss*, which is selling a stock for less than you paid.) The importance of understanding a drawdown is that it shows the full extent of a market drop. In 2008, the S&P 500 stock market index fell 38%, the worst in seven decades. But from the high to low—peak to trough—the drawdown was 50%. A relative returns investor whose account balance declined "only" 25% suddenly isn't happy about a *relative* 13% return (38% market average drop versus investor's 25% drawdown equals a 13% relative return). She now wants all the upside and none of the drawdowns, low-volatility absolute returns with high-volatility relative returns. Who wouldn't? But that's not reality.

Similarly, a relative returns investor is an absolute returns investor disappointed when the market zooms. Absolutists endured schoolyard taunts from relativists whose accounts ballooned in the 1984–2000 bull market. Eventually the absolutists, tired of the bullying, chased high-volatility returns other folks were enjoying, and many made the switch at the worst time.

All else equal, higher returns require enduring higher volatility, and lower volatility demands accepting lower returns. And the returns everyone else is getting—market index returns—require accepting the volatility everyone else receives, whatever it is.

TABLE 2.2 Absolute or Relative Returns, Not Both

WHAT IS POSSIBLE?	HIGHER EXPECTED RETURNS THAN MARKET INDEXES	LOWER EXPECTED RETURNS THAN MARKET INDEXES
HIGHER VOLATILITY	More likely if using 6 tests (Laid out in Chapters 4 and 5) (RELATIVE RETURNS)	Sure, easy to lose money if speculating ("taking a flyer")!
LOWER VOLATILITY	NOT POSSIBLE	Likely (ABSOLUTE RETURNS)

It doesn't matter which you pursue—absolute, relative or market index returns—but once you make the choice, *stick to it*. Use the right tool for the right job.

THE PROBLEM WITH ALL BENCHMARKS

The best way to measure your investing success is not by whether you're beating the market but by whether you've put in place a financial plan and a behavioral discipline that are likely to get you where you want to go.

——BENJAMIN GRAHAM

If you are going to be a relative returns investor, what will your results be relative *to*? And should you be relative at all?

The common tool for measuring performance—what to benchmark against- is the S&P 500. The thinking goes, "Well, I could always have the market's average return, so everything else must be measured against it," where "it" is a low-cost index fund that mimics the S&P 500. So the idea is that anything else than investing in that fund is the opportunity cost (Chapter 1). While the S&P 500 is the most common benchmark, it is not the only one, nor is it the best.

TABLE 2.3 Representative Performance Benchmarks

INDEX	BENCHMARK BEST FOR . . .	COMPANIES (About 5,000 publicly traded in the U.S., down from 9,000 in 1997)	WEIGHTED OR AVERAGE
S&P 500	U.S. large caps. Not representative of entire market, especially small stocks	500 large companies	Weighted, 10 companies—2%!—largely determine the movement of the index
Nasdaq 100	U.S. large caps traded on the Nasdaq (National Association of Securities Dealers Automated Quotations)	Top 100 companies by market value traded on the Nasdaq Exchange	Weighted
Dow Jones Industrial Average	Only the stocks in the average	30, wide range, excludes utilities and transportation (DJ has own indexes for those)	Weighted (despite being named an "average")
Wilshire 5000 Total Market Index	U.S. broad market	5000	Weighted
Russell 2000	U.S. small caps	2000 smallest of Russell 3000 index companies	Weighted
MSCI EAFE (Europe Australia Far East)	Stocks in developed markets outside U.S. and Canada	Varies, currently 925	Weighted
NYSE Composite	U.S. large caps traded on the New York Stock Exchange	All stocks traded on the New York Stock Exchange, currently 2,750	Weighted

The S&P 500 is an index of 500 large companies in the United States. A "publicly traded company" is one whose shares you can buy and sell on a stock exchange (you don't have to find a buyer on the street somewhere, which happened in the early days of the exchanges, where some people would even buy and sell on the street's curb). Also, "largest" doesn't mean stock price. The S&P 500 people don't average Apple's $100 stock price, Priceline's $1,230, General Electric's $30, and Amazon's $638, for example, or weight by sales, earnings per share, cash flows, or Mercedes in the parking lots.

> **Did you know...**
> That the S&P 500 is named for Henry Varnum Poor. "Poor" is *not* a good name for anyone in finance, but we can't blame him for this accident of birth. Happily for him, he prospered despite the name. In 1860, Ol' Henry started the investment research business eventually known as Standard & Poor's. Many identities later, it's a division of publisher McGraw-Hill and offers the well-known S&P 500 index.

The S&P 500 and all of the benchmarks in the table are weighted by company market value, or the more common "market capitalization" or "market cap". Market cap is a company's shares times its stock price. There are 5.5 billion Apple shares and the stock price is currently $100, so the market cap is $550 billion dollars. The larger and more profitable the business, the more demand for shares, the more shares and/or higher price, the larger the market cap. Voilà, Apple has the highest market cap of any company in the world.

Because the S&P 500 weights companies, 10 mega market cap companies like Apple—*a mere 2%* of the S&P's 500 companies—largely determine the direction of the index. To understand the effect, if you took Facebook, Amazon, Alphabet (Google) and (not top 10 but familiar brand) Netflix out of the S&P 500, the index would change from the reported *slight gain* in the first quarter of 2016 to *down about 6%*! That's a huge difference. In short, the big bullies run the schoolyard. The S&P 500 bullies today are:

TABLE 2.4 The Top 10 Companies That Dominate the S&P 500

RANK	COMPANY	MARKET CAP (billions)	BUSINESS	COMPARABLE COUNTRY GDP
1	Apple	$550	iEverything!	Switzerland, Saudi Arabia
2	Microsoft	$411	Windows operating systems for PCs, Xbox, Skype, mobile phone operating systems, Bing	Belgium, Poland, Norway
3	ExxonMobil	$378	Energy	United Arab Emirates, South Africa
4	Berkshire Hathaway	$351	Warren Buffet's mega-conglomerate	
5	General Electric	$309	Manufacturing conglomerate	Hong Kong, Philippines, Israel, Singapore, Denmark
6	Amazon	$300	The Everything Store	
7	Facebook	$290	Can't live with it, can't live without it	
8	Well Fargo	$281	Diversified financial services company	
9	Johnson & Johnson	$278	Diversified healthcare businesses	Colombia, Pakistan
10	JP Morgan Chase	$243	Diversified financial behemoth	Chile

SOURCES: us.spindices.com, Wikipedia, knoema.com.

Great, so you can always get that return in an S&P 500 index fund, but do you want to own, in effect, these large companies, because you would. Through any number of investment options, most of us own the top 10 whether we know it or not. If you have a government retirement plan, employer plan, or mutual funds your uncle Ted left you, they own the indexes and/or its biggest stocks. This is why diversification through the S&P 500 index is something of a mirage. It's a poor measure of opportunity cost and not the right benchmark for everyone's investments.

> *Did you know...*
> Another serious problem with using the indexes to benchmark is that they suffer from **survivorship bias.** They do not account for companies falling off due to poor performance, which reduces the companies' market values and drops them off the index. (They are simply replaced by others.) This is a major problem with, say, mutual fund industry overall performance and rankings. Poor performing funds lose investors and close. So the oft-cited statistic that about 75% of actively-managed mutual funds fail to outperform the S&P 500 over five years or more is actually worse because it excludes those that do not survive!

If you talk to people about their saving and investing goals, the smart ones don't care about "beating the market." If they want market index returns they can use a low-cost index fund that tracks the Wilshire 5000, for example, add new money regularly and reinvest the dividends. It's all about what kind of drawdowns (remember that's a large drop from peak to trough as opposed to a loss, which only occurs upon selling) you are willing to accept over determined periods. Most people want to

Diversification through the S&P 500 index is something of a mirage. It's a poor measure of opportunity cost and not the right benchmark for everyone's investments.

know that, within reason, their money will meet or beat inflation and grow some between now and retirement. For them, perhaps the best benchmark of opportunity cost is the Consumer Price Index (CPI).

Lastly, the rearview mirror is insidious. People have a tendency to look back wistfully at, say, Apple, with "If only I had bought it in the teens when it had more than half of that in cash!" At that time, Apple stock offered a serious risk of losing investor money. It was not profitable, and iEverything did not exist. You might have seen a techie geek with an iPod, but if you tried it—hey, it didn't even have instructions! The catch is that the company we know today is a different one than over a decade ago. Using today to judge a decision in the past is *hindsight bias*. Seriously, did you *know* Apple—or any stock—was going to go up? Plus, how much would you have invested? Would you have kept the stock forever or sold after some gains? And in between there are myriad other decisions.

All we can do is use information today to estimate our results in the unknown future. We can't control what happens, but we can control our investment decision-making process. The key is to make an intelligent decision about strategy and stick to it.

The key is to make an intelligent decision about strategy and stick to it, not worry about the benchmark.

The biggest danger isn't in picking an index as a benchmark and using that to gauge your opportunity cost, but rather it's in not knowing *why* you are doing that, *what* strategy you are using, and *whether* it is being consistently applied. Chapters 4 and 5 are what this book recommends, but it doesn't matter what you choose so long as you are patient and persevere. Be sturdy in the stock market storm, not adrift in the open seas.

CHECK YOUR KNOWLEDGE #4

"Stock market indexes like the S&P 500 and Wilshire 5000 show the performance of the average stock in the index."

NEVER. *Most commonly used indexes are actually weighted by a company's market value. Apple, currently #1 in the S&P 500, is weighted ("counts") many many times more than the 500th largest company in the index.*

LYNCHED: YOUR CIRCLE OF COMPETENCE

I'm no genius. I'm smart in spots—but I stay around those spots.

—**TOM WATSON SR.**, *Founder of IBM*

All value investing—this book's core philosophy for non-index (active) investing—requires knowing your circle of competence. In other words: What do you *think* you know, compared to what you *really* know? While we push ourselves to learn more and more, we truly know few, if any, businesses so well that we can evaluate their suitability for investment. You can know businesses such as ones you work for. What do they make or services do they provide, how well have they done, and who is their competition? In fact, all of us know some kind of business but not many businesses, if we think about it.

But circle of competence is often misinterpreted. Peter Lynch's book *One Up On Wall Street* is a justly classic primer for investors. However, like all holy books, whether investing, economics, or religion, its teachings are often taken out of context. Decades of readers have misunderstood his famous "buy what you know" dictum as suggesting one should make investment decisions this way: "*I eat at Bob Evans, use Microsoft Of-*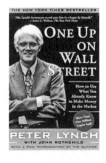

fice/Google Search/Apple iPhone, drink Sam Adams, so I'll buy their stocks!"

> **Did you know…**
> As the manager of the Magellan Fund at Fidelity Investments between 1977 and 1990, Peter Lynch averaged a 29.2% annual return, consistently more than doubling the S&P 500 market index and making it the best performing mutual fund in the world.
>
> **SOURCE:** Wikipedia

Friends, this is not what "buy what you know" means. To know the *product* is not to know the *business*. It could have too much debt, issue too many stock options that dilute our ownership, face increasing competition, pursue unwise new business ventures, and worse. Many investors thought they "bought what they knew" with Einstein's Bagels, Boston Chicken, Crazy Eddie's, East-

Many investors thought they "bought what they knew" with Einstein's Bagels, Boston Chicken, Crazy Eddie's, Eastman Kodak, General Motors as well as many airlines, but they all went bankrupt.

man Kodak, General Motors, as well as many airlines, but they all went bankrupt. The Farnam Street blog shows it this way:

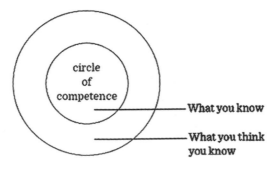

FIGURE 2.7

To stay within your circle of competence—to buy what you know—means to use your expertise to buy businesses you understand deeply. Those about which you could tell someone in a minute how they make money, how they make more of it, what they do with the money they make, and whether they are in good financial shape with cash, debt, and competition. If you can't do it—and most can't—don't buy the stock. Grab a low-cost index fund from Vanguard or find a fairly-priced investment (not financial) advisor, but don't kid yourself if a stock you see is not a business within your circle of competence. Incompetence loses money.

LIVING (AND DYING) ON THE MARGIN

Elevator operators and secretaries were buying on margin!
—**ROBERT JACOBS,** *Tom's father, describing the run-up to the Crash of 1929*

Brokerage firms will gladly lend you money and charge you interest to buy and own stocks. This is called "buying on margin." Investors use margin because it can boost returns. Let's say you pay $8,000 in cash and use an $8,000 margin loan to buy $16,000 worth of Blast Off Stock. Blast Off does indeed zoom so that your stake is worth $24,000. That's a 50% gain from $16,000 to $24,000, right?

Wrong!

You actually made 100%. If you sell for $24,000 and repay the $8,000 loan, you receive $16,000, putting aside taxes and margin interest. That's *double* your $8,000, so your "cash-on-cash return" is 100%. You risked $8,000 to make $8,000. This is why margin is so alluring when stock prices are rising. Borrowing to buy stock—buying on margin—magnifies returns on the way up.

> *Borrowing to buy stock—buying on margin—magnifies returns on the way up. But it may also destroy you on the way down.*

But it may also destroy you on the way down. Investors buying on margin—the "elevator operators and secretaries" of Tom's father's Crash of 1929 stories—eventually learn that easy money today can kill you tomorrow when the market plummets.

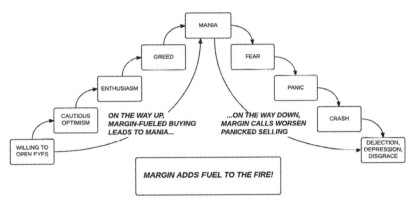

FIGURE 2.8

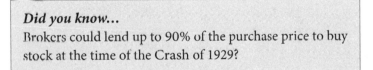

Did you know...
Brokers could lend up to 90% of the purchase price to buy stock at the time of the Crash of 1929?

In the U.S., Federal Reserve Regulation T allows brokerage firms to lend up to, but no more than, 50% of the stock purchase price. Then, each broker requires investors to maintain ("maintenance requirement") from 25% to as much as 40% equity in the account. "Equity" is the same as equity in your home: its sales price today minus mortgage debt outstanding. If your house would sell today for $300,000 and your loan balance is $120,000, you have $180,000 in equity. Similarly, your brokerage account equity is the value today of your securities ("house") minus the margin loan from your broker ("mortgage").

Now assume that Blast Off Stock, as usually happens, returns to earth. Instead of rising to $24,000, your holding declines to $12,000.

Your equity is $4,000 ($12,000 value of stock minus the $8,000 margin loan). You exceed a 25% maintenance requirement, which would be $3,000. Good. But if the requirement at your brokerage firm is 40%, or $4,800, you lack enough equity. In that case, you will receive a "margin call" to deposit cash or securities into your account—and/or sell stocks—to return to the 40% equity level.

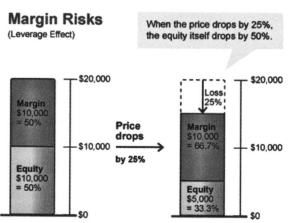

FIGURE 2.9 Source: https://www.firstrade.com/content/en-us/education/margin/marginrisks

The deeper the decline, the more investors receive margin calls. With everyone selling to raise equity, stocks plummet and bring further margin calls, sales and losses. This is the vicious cycle, the opposite of the virtuous one, and it explains partly why market drops can happen and worsen in no time. Before you can say "Time for Netflix!" you may have a full-fledged screaming bloody crash on your hands. People, financial institutions and whole economies are devastated.

Most of us buy houses and cars on margin, though we call it a mortgage or loan. From 2003 to the 2008 crash in the U.S., borrowing fueled speculation in real estate and stocks, where new paper profits fueled more debt, and round and round. Eventually lending froze, debt-fueled profit evaporated, and we endured the housing bust and the Great Recession. However, where lenders could only foreclose on the house or may repossess your car (as in the classic film *Repo Man*), margin loans are different. The brokerage firm can sell anything in your account without warning and you are responsible for any balance owed:

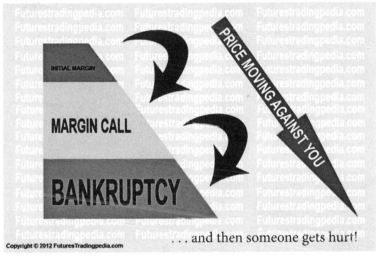

FIGURE 2.10

All manias are fueled by credit, and margin is credit. All panics become crashes when the debt comes due. It's a cycle as sure as death and taxes. Margin may look good today, but it can kill you tomorrow. Do not a margin borrower be.

CHAPTER 3

Fortune Favors the Prepared Mind

The investor's chief problem—and even his worst enemy—is likely to be himself.

—BENJAMIN GRAHAM

MENTAL ACCOUNTING

. . . the odd mental gymnastics we put ourselves through to rationalize spending or saving in particular ways. We see money in vastly different ways based on where it came from and to what use we wish to put it.

—JAMES SUROWIECKI

Investing isn't about beating others at their game. It's about controlling yourself at your own game.

—BENJAMIN GRAHAM

There's a reason that they say it's better to be lucky than smart. To see luck—to recognize it right in front of us—the mind must be sharp and rational. Most of us miss what's right in front of us because we are busy with emotions. We can't see luck if we are unprepared, but we can develop *the prepared mind*. We can overcome our tendency to allow personalities and emotions to push us towards irrational investment decisions. *We* are our own biggest obstacles.

Challenge number one is "mental accounting." You find a $10 bill on the street. How do you feel? Maybe you take a quick glance around to see if it might belong to anyone, but then, you realize it's free money! Woohoo! The brain clicks into immediate gratification mode. This is our animal side. We are wired for the adrenaline rush of now, and the immediate desire to spend it!

The rational thing to do is deposit the $10 into a checking account and spend it according to your budget. We don't do that. Real people practice mental accounting. We often apply *subjective, not objective* criteria to money. In his breakthrough paper, Richard Thaler gives several examples, the first of himself:

> *A few years ago I gave a talk to a group of executives in Switzerland. After the conference my wife and I spent a week visiting the area. At that time the Swiss franc was at an all-time high relative to the U.S. dollar, so the usual high prices in Switzerland were astronomical. My wife and I comforted ourselves that I had received a fee for the talk that would easily cover the outrageous prices for hotels and meals. Had I received the same fee a week earlier for a talk in New York though, the vacation would have been much less enjoyable.*

Assuming the amount paid in francs to be the same in dollars, it shouldn't matter where he was paid the same amount. Thaler in his example—and anyone practicing mental accounting—violates the principle that a dollar is *fungible*: Any U.S. dollar has the same value as and may be exchanged for any other U.S. dollar. There is no advantage or difference between one dollar bill and another. Yet "mental accounting" drops the

Thaler in his example—and anyone practicing mental accounting—violates the principle that a dollar is fungible: *Any U.S. dollar has the same value as and may be exchanged for any other U.S. dollar.*

Swiss fee into a different category than a New York fee, just as we commonly place the *found* $10 in a different bucket than an *earned* $10.

More humorous but equally telling is Thaler's next and more extreme tale:

> *A friend of mine was once shopping for a quilted bedspread. She went to a department store and was pleased to find a model she liked on sale. The spreads came in three sizes: double, queen and king. The usual prices for these quilts were $200, $250 and $300 respectively, but during the sale they were all priced at only $150. My friend bought the king-size quilt and was quite pleased with her purchase, though the quilt did hang a bit over the sides of her double bed.*

She is going to pay $150 no matter what, but she "accounts" for the higher savings for the king and buys it, even though it doesn't fit her bed!

Take credit card use. We may have credit card debt costing us 15% interest per year, yet at the same time we have a vacation, entertainment or other fun fund growing each year, too. Think of it as putting all your change in a jar, taking it to the bank each year and treating yourself to a dinner out, even though you carry a high interest credit card balance month-to-month. That is considered irrational, even though to some it seems very rational. Truth is, it would be rational if, instead of putting money in the jar, you used those savings to pay down your debt, which gives you an immediate gain in terms of your card's interest rate. So if that rate is 15%, that's a 15 cent savings on each dollar paid for every year you'd have that debt. You can't make that kind of money easily (or legally)! But that reward is distant, while the money for the vacation is here *now*. Yes, it may feel good today, but tomorrow the debt grows heavier.

> **Did you know...**
> The average credit card debt per U.S. household
> in March 2016 was $5,700. But if you exclude the
> households that pay off their balance every month, the
> average approaches three times more—$16,048!
>
> SOURCE: http://www.valuepenguin.com/average-credit-card-debt

Lots of investors practice mental accounting. They divide their investment cash into lower risk stocks and then take a smaller amount for "a flyer" on something sexy, speculative—fun! Fun!? *Really?* Would they take the same money and go to the casino or buy lotto tickets? That's what they're doing. Over time, this will reduce overall investment gains.

Mental Accounting

The rational choices are clear, but we often fail to make them. Therefore, Thaler has become a major advocate for forced savings, through a nudge, not a hammer. Because the traditional pension is long gone, people must save and invest for their own retirement, most often through a company plan like a 401(k). But participation rates in these plans remain far below 100%, even though money contributed is before tax—thus earns an immediate profit of your tax rate (33%, say)—and the company often matches your contributions! Thaler and Cass Sunstein in their 2008 book *Nudge* cite research suggesting that an "opt-out" (you're included in the 401(k) plan at some low percentage of income unless you request to be out) rather than "opt-in" (you're not in the plan unless you request to be in) policy dramatically increases participation. Research showed that under the opt-in approach for new employees, participation rates were 20% after 3 months of employment, and gradually increased to 65%

after 36 months. "But when automatic enrollment ["opt-out"] was adopted, enrollment of new employees jumped to 90% immediately and increased to more than 98% within 36 months." Sometimes we require a nudge.

Life would be a colossal bore if we only made entirely rational financial decisions. After all, we earn psychic income—non-monetary benefits—from spending our money on dates, birthday gifts or charitable donations, for example, despite the opportunity costs. So life is a balance, living in the present while saving and investing for the future. The Red Queen tells Alice in *Alice Through the Looking Glass*, "The rule is, jam tomorrow and jam yesterday, but never jam today."

Not so. We *can* have jam today, but if we also save and invest, we'll have more jam tomorrow.

THE HEEBNER JEEBIES: BUYING HIGH, SELLING LOW

Never buy a stock because it has gone up or sell one because it has gone down.
——BENJAMIN GRAHAM

The prepared mind must tune out the financial media and make no investing decisions based on them. Paying attention to financial entertainers like Jim Cramer is the surest route to buying high, selling low, and losing money permanently.

Whenever there is a quick significant drop in the broad market indexes—and they are almost always not gradual—the financial news media would have you believe the world is coming to an end. They appeal to our emotions to attract our eyes and ears to sell to advertisers. Calm is *not* good for business—people might actually move their attention elsewhere. That's why Chicken Little is a big winner for the media.

The financial world understands that people fear market drops, so it exaggerates short-term market movements to hook us. Eventually, assaulted by enough weeping, wailing, and gnashing of teeth, investors sell. They lock in losses. Then, in roaring markets, ebullient news coverage leads greedy investors to buy en masse, usually just in time for stocks to crash to earth.

Buying high and selling low guarantee losses, and no one knows when markets will turn. That's why successful investing is not about *timing* the markets, but *time in* the markets. Profits come

> *Successful investing is not about* timing *the markets, but* time in *the markets.*

to those who stay the course, invest regularly and automatically, and steel themselves to ride out the short-term—and often quite jarring—paper gains and losses in their accounts. Unfortunately, because no one has repealed human nature, this is tough to do.

Mutual fund rating company Morningstar studied this phenomenon. It examined one of the most successful funds of all time, the CGM Focus Fund. Its manager, Ken Heebner, is little known outside of a small circle of investing nerds, where he is a legend. Morningstar examined CGM's return from January 2000, just before the devastating 2000–02 crash began, to March 25, 2010, a year after the crash of 2008–09 ended. Despite choosing a period including the two worst bear markets since 1973–74, CGM delivered average annual returns of 18%, which is astonishing. It doubled money every four years! Despite the booms and busts, someone who invested at almost any point and stayed the course would have done quite well with Heebner.

Unfortunately, most CGM Focus Fund investors did not stay the course. Instead, they behaved like . . . people. For example, they poured money into the CGM Focus Fund *after* Heebner's 80% gain in 2007, just in time for the fund's 48% swoon in 2008. Morningstar found that typical investors during this period actually *lost* 11% per year, despite CGM's 18% annualized gains! Selling in downturns and buying in upturns, they let emotion lead them to time the markets, not stay in them. Not good.

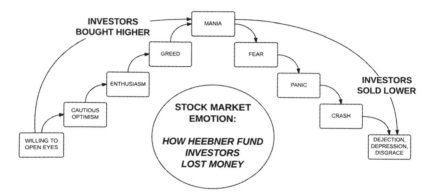

FIGURE 3.1

Be the investor with a prepared mind. If you invest regularly at all, such as in an employer plan, keep doing it. Don't jump from fund to fund based on last year's results. Don't let the financial media play upon your emotions to lead you to bad decisions. Let others get the Heebner Jeebies and buy what was hot last year, selling what was cold. They won't enjoy the long-term returns available in the market, but you will.

CHECK YOUR KNOWLEDGE #5

"When choosing among the mutual funds your company offers in your 401(k) or other plan, it's smart to choose the funds that did best last year and sell those that performed poorly."

NEVER. *This usually results in buying high and selling low. Provided that the manager has a good track record over years—not last year—it's actually best to buy soon after a bad year.*

AGREE TO DISAGREE

Just because someone agrees with you doesn't mean you're right.

——**ZINTIS,** *Tom's nephew, when in high school, to his uncle*

A man hears what he wants to hear, and disregards the rest.

——**"THE BOXER,"** *by Paul Simon*

When everyone agrees with me it's time for me to quit.

—— **PHIL LADUKE,** *Safety Consultant*

The most common obstacle to having a prepared mind is this: It's human nature to look for sources that reinforce our positions, decisions, and actions and to filter out all except what confirms our views.

We tend to surround ourselves with people and media who think as we do to reinforce the view that we are right, whoever we are and whatever the subject may be. In fact, there is evidence that on social media platforms, people are generally reluctant to share opinions for fear of being different and causing discord.

> Human nature is to filter out all except what confirms our views.

Did you know...

Contrary to conventional wisdom, there is no evidence that the famous economist John Maynard Keynes actually said, "When my information changes, I alter my conclusions. What do you do, sir?" But there is an apt and funny story about a telegram exchange between Keynes and British Prime Minister Winston Churchill in 1945: Churchill cabled Keynes, "Am coming around to your point of view." Keynes replied, "Sorry to hear it. Have started to change my mind." (Whether it too is true, we cannot say.)

SOURCE: http://quoteinvestigator.com/2011/07/22/keynes-change-mind/

The general practice is that whenever there is a dominant opinion on something in your community—however defined—go along or be quiet. Most people don't really want to hear views that don't confirm theirs; we are prone to confirmation bias. The more public we are with our views, the harder it is to change them, because we would look inconsistent and maybe offend those with whom we had agreed. Emerson may have been right in theory when he wrote, "A foolish consistency is the hobgoblin of little minds," but in practice, hobgoblins are everywhere. They are easier and comforting.

This is one reason many advisors and managers don't write or speak publicly about stocks they own. The minute we do, there is an unwritten human law that every recipient expects us to be "right," even though all investing is about handicapping probabilities of an uncertain future. There will always be good results and poor ones. The sage value investor Guy Spear says he never talks about his holdings in public to be better able to sell a stock any time for his clients' welfare without appearing inconsistent or even flighty. It's like sex in high school. The more teens brag about it, the less likely they're having it. The best advisors and managers aren't all over the media. They're making better decisions privately to make money for clients.

We must review our decisions whenever the facts change. That requires avoiding confirmation bias and seeking out contrary opinions. We must listen to opposing viewpoints that are sensible, backed up by facts, and dare we say "civil?" Being fair to the other side only makes our investment and life decisions better.

THE UNPOPULARITY CONTEST

Go where . . . you can get an advantage and where there are fewer people looking at the stocks. Go where the competition is low.

——CHARLIE MUNGER, *Vice-Chairman, Berkshire Hathaway*

We have not known a single person who has consistently or lastingly made money by thus 'following the market'. We do not hesitate to declare this approach as fallacious as it is popular.

——BENJAMIN GRAHAM

Now that we know to avoid confirmation bias—the tendency to seek out and accept only views that agree with ours—it's time to find the places where investors fear to tread. The prepared mind knows the answer to this question: Which race are you most likely to win— one where you greet the starting gun with few to no competitors, or another in which a field is packed with racers side-to-side and back 50 rows? The answer is obvious, and yet almost everyone makes the wrong choice.

Li Ka-shing is practically unknown outside of Asia, yet he is a brilliant value investor whose Cheung Kong Holdings and Hutchison Whampoa holding companies have earned him the moniker "Asia's Warren Buffett." His son Victor has not fallen far from the tree, as we see in a commencement address he gave:

It is difficult to succeed or to maintain your fruits of success if you do not look long-term. Do not get me wrong—be it long or short-term, profit is always good. But short-term profit is almost too much fun, too many people like it—as a result, the scene is usually crowded and competition is keen. On the other hand, **"It is difficult to succeed or to maintain your fruits of success if you do not look long-term." —Victor Li, son of Hong Kong billionaire value investor Li Ka-shing.** *long-term investment needs patience and hard work. The process involves several up and down cycles and is usually less exciting. As a result, most people do not enjoy it as much and the competition scene is less crowded. Wonderful news for those who prefer the longer process.*

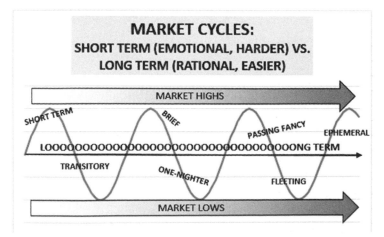

FIGURE 3.2

But what is "long-term?" This is frequently misunderstood. Most people think it means buying something and holding it nearly forever. Not so for value investors such as Li father and son. It means buying cheaply or not at all. It means having the patience to wait for desperate sellers, buy from them, and hold until buyers will pay any price to take the stock off your hands. It can take time and be really (really) boring in a world today where U.S. investors see companies zoom to absurd valuations overnight. Those anxious investors say, "I'm getting left behind! Get on the train!"

Victor Li observes that short-term profit is more fun. No wonder the media love to tell us about the overnight stock successes, not the thousand that flame out. The latter don't make good stories. The problem with news is that what sells—what grabs our attention so that the media outlets can sell our eyes and ears to advertisers—is so consistent that we overestimate the frequency of the reported events. We are transfixed by endless reporting of massive disasters and worry about them happening to us, even though the odds may be infinitesimal. This is called the "availability heuristic." We overestimate the frequency of events that are easy to recall, and disasters and quick fortunes are very memorable. The prepared mind is wary of this trap.

> *Did you know...*
> Walmart does not have the most retail stores in the world, with 11,620. That honor belongs to the all-but unknown A.S. Watson group, controlled by Li Ka-shing's companies, with 12,500 stores. Unlike Walmart, A.S. Watson uses or buys store names familiar in the country where they operate, rather than the same name worldwide. But like Walmart, it uses a worldwide supply chain to lower costs and improve profits.

There is no such thing as a free lunch or a fast buck. Li's father bought cheap land from British residents fleeing Hong Kong in 1967 during riots by sympathizers with Mainland China's Cultural Revolution under Mao. It was gutsy, but he believed one thing: Hong Kong had a terrific location and no room for development, and China would likely not risk a war with the U.K. when its own economy was being devastated. Military action against a great power and its allies costs money, which China did not have. Li has patiently developed that land for 48 years. His decision took a long time to lead to profits.

> *Did you know...*
> Ironically, the unrest that allowed Li Ka-shing to buy land cheaply in Hong Kong originated with a labor dispute at *his own* artificial flower factory!

Victor Li's simple advice is that to be long-term—to think in terms of and live through several economic and market cycles—is an advantage. Perhaps it's not as much fun as a fast buck, but it's the way to go.

RECENCY BIAS

Invert, always invert!

——**CHARLIE MUNGER,** *Vice-Chairman of Berkshire Hathaway*

Imagine this: It's rained like crazy for months, so we think it will continue, the drought is gone for good, and farmers should plant more this year. Or, the economy is growing and will continue to grow, therefore credit and consumption will expand. Housing prices are rising, they will always increase, so it's required to buy a house any-where at any price now. The bull market's lasted six years, it will keep on stampeding, invest more today! On the negative side, we might believe that the current war, drought, or recession will never end and crushed stocks will go to zero. People project both good times and bad times into the future.

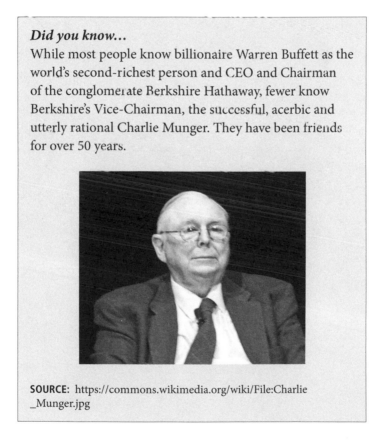

Did you know...
While most people know billionaire Warren Buffett as the world's second-richest person and CEO and Chairman of the conglomerate Berkshire Hathaway, fewer know Berkshire's Vice-Chairman, the successful, acerbic and utterly rational Charlie Munger. They have been friends for over 50 years.

SOURCE: https://commons.wikimedia.org/wiki/File:Charlie_Munger.jpg

This human behavioral tendency is *recency bias*. We think whatever is recent will continue. It can, but not indefinitely. The longer some-thing continues to be the same, the more likely it is to change (as in Chapter 2's "Time Wounds All Heels"). Once upon a time, the Democrats controlled both houses of Congress for what seemed like forever. Then things changed. Just as it seemed inconceivable then to have a Republican House of Representatives, now it seems unimaginable to have a Democratic one.

Another example. The revolution in telecommunications we know today was inconceivable before 1984. AT&T was a legal monopoly, the only choice for phone service. AT&T owned the wires to your home and the equipment you used. Heck, the Princess phone, let alone push button dialing, was a revolution! You couldn't legally attach any equipment to your phone, not even an answering machine. Then poof! A judicial order ended the monopoly in 1984 and largely unleashed the telecom revolution of widespread mobile and Internet communications. *What happened yesterday and what happens today may be completely different tomorrow.*

RECENCY BIAS

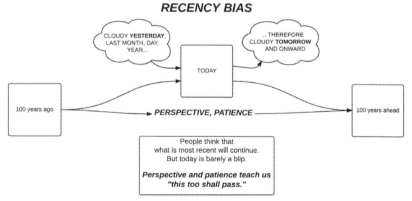

FIGURE 3.3

Recency bias causes poor investing decisions. The progression of stock markets is a cycle of dejection, recovery, enthusiasm, mania, panic, crash, and around again. As Victor Li observed, few pay attention long enough to see *even one* full market cycle. Rather, they see only the recent and current environment. This is why investors tend to buy high at times of great enthusiasm—mania—and sell out at times of fear—panic and crash. They lack patience and perspective.

If we know that market cycles exist, we keep some cash on hand and wait. When euphoria reigns, we're wary of new investments. When dejection is the rule, we put that cash to use. Don't we want to be the people with cash when stocks go on sale, just as we choose to shop? Yes, maybe the sale will be better next month, or prices may indeed go up next month, but market cycles will always exist in a capitalist system. Knowing the wheel of mania, panic and crash allows us to have the perspective to avoid recency bias.

> "The intelligent investor is a realist who sells to optimists and buys from pessimists."
> —Benjamin Graham

Warren Buffett says to "be fearful when others are greedy and greedy when others are fearful." His partner at Berkshire Hathaway, Charlie Munger, further applies that principle to all sound reasoning: "Invert, always invert." What if the opposite of what we believe is true? What if Buddhism and *Streetcar Named Desire* are right that life or what we believe is an illusion? How does this affect our attitudes toward risk and reward?

The prepared mind fights recency bias to make the most well-informed and profitable decisions we can, given an unknown future. "Invert, always invert." Sorry Shakespeare, but the past is rarely prologue.

PERCENTAGES, NOT POINTS

A journalist is supposed to present an unbiased portrait of an event, a view devoid of intimate emotions. This is impossible, of course. The framing of an image, by its very composition, represents a choice. The photographer chooses what to show and what to exclude.

—ALEXANDRA KERRY

Here is a test. Which of these lines is longer?

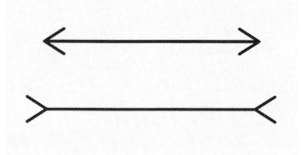

FIGURE 3.4

If you say the bottom line, you are like most everyone else. The lines are the same length, but the arrows on the top line and tails on the bottom line create the illusion that the latter is longer. This is the Müller-Lyer illusion of 1889. It shows that how information is presented to us affects our decisions and shows *framing bias,* the tendency to behave differently depending on how a situation is presented to us.

> **Did you know...**
> Political "spin" is nothing more than the attempt to frame an issue so that voters will see an issue the spinner's way.

Charts frame stock performance too and may mislead us. The linear chart uses points, which leads us to think that stock price gains are all the same. The logarithmic chart is more accurate, showing the percentage gains. Almost all authorities in the media offer the point, not percentage, change in market indexes. Even the gold standard PBS NewsHour reports *points* Monday through Thursday and *percentages* only on Friday. But the prepared mind focuses on percentages, not points.

Using the familiar stock market index of the largest 500 companies, Points People look at the world like this:

S&P 500: 1960–2/19/2016 LINEAR
(gray columns are U.S. recessions)

EQUAL SPACING
VERTICAL AXIS

B LINEAR: +1183 points

A LINEAR: +114 points

FIGURE 3.5 Source: YCharts

Points People sigh with boredom at a mere 114-point rise from 1960 to mid-1985. Flat as Kansas, not making you any money, right? But wow, the bull market from March 2009 to today brought an 1183-point rocket, just over *ten times 114*. Points People think that grows their wallets bigger than a waistline in Pie Town! Linear charts accomplish this through an *equidistant* horizontal axis.

Not so fast. While the second period's gains were 1183 points more than the first period's, *percentage gains were exactly the same: 161%.* Yup. Percentage People see it like this:

S&P 500: 1960–2/19/2016 LOGARITHMIC
(gray columns are U.S. recessions)

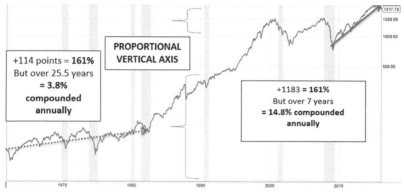

FIGURE 3.6 Source: YCharts

Unlike the linear chart, the log chart recognizes that points are not created equal. Here, the numbers on the right show that the lower the starting point, the more a few points really boost percentage. When the numbers are larger, the same amount of points gained produces a smaller percentage jump. From 500 to 1,000 is 100%, but 1,000 to 1,500 is 50%. The logarithmic chart shows this with a *proportional* horizontal axis.

But wait, there's more. If the percentages are the same, why don't the two gains—the two arrows—rise at the same angle? *Because time matters.* Yes, the 161% total returns are identical, but the first takes 25.5 years and the second just under 7 years. So which would you prefer? The latter is more appealing, and to explain that, we must express the *total* return (161%) as a function of *time.* That's *annualized* return. Earning a sleepy 3.8% annually for 25.5 years leads to

161%; if you reap 161% in just under 7 years, you enjoy 14.8% annualized. Same total return, different annualized return. In a log chart, a steeper slope indicates a shorter time period for the gain. And the narrower the horizontal lines—here 1,000 to 1,500 is narrower than 500 to 1,000—the lower the percentage gain.

All this said, there are three main takeaways regarding looking at any chart purporting to show stock market or individual stock performance:

1. Percentages, not points, matter.
2. Log charts, not linear, tell the story.
3. Time matters, so count annualized (compounded annual) gains, not calendar year (annual) gains.
4. Watch out for any framing bias in the way information is presented.

The moral of the story is that the prepared mind questions authority, especially when anyone presents numbers. Straighten the pictures.

MANAGE EMOTIONS THROUGH DCA

By developing your discipline and courage, you can refuse to let other people's mood swings govern your financial destiny. In the end, how your investments behave is much less important than how you behave.

——BENJAMIN GRAHAM

We know that the prepared investing mind must manage emotions. Otherwise, when markets are low and investor sentiment depressed, we are more likely to sell at the wrong time. And when they are high and manic, we dive in. This is guaranteed to lose money. Once again to the market cycle:

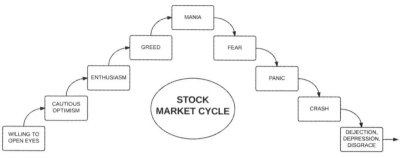

FIGURE 3.7

Fortunately, there is a handy tool to manage emotion: dollar-cost averaging (DCA). It's simple—you likely are already doing it—but as we'll see, it takes a prepared mind.

DCA is a strategy for investing an amount of money every set period. For example, if your employer has a retirement plan, you probably contribute each paycheck and never waver. Or, if you are saving and investing on your own or get professional advice, you likely do the same thing. Setting up an automatic payment to go from your checking account to your investment account each set period puts your investing on autopilot, preventing emotion from pushing you off course.

By averaging your purchases over time, you smooth out the normal ups and downs of the stock market. You don't have to care whether it's 2008 (ouch), 1995–2000 (zoom zoom), and so on. Disciplined dollar-cost averaging, if strictly adhered to, can take emotion out of investing. You stay on the yellow brick road despite the monkeys and Wicked Witch of the stock market pulling you in one direction and the glitter and promise of the Emerald City pulling you to the other.

Mutual funds—entities that buy baskets of stocks—are the most common options in employer retirement accounts. Therefore, they are the most common investments for individuals. Let's take some Monopoly® money and see what could happen if we invested $100 a month in a mythical mutual fund trading between $30 and $74 over 24 months.

FIGURE 3.8

Note the solid line for Average Price Paid. The investor who perseveres, investing $100 a month without fail, maintains a steady price paid even though the mutual fund itself—reflecting the stock market it invests in—bungees all over the place. But the investor must not sell in despair in month 13 when losses on paper mount, because the $100 buys *more shares at a lower price* and average price declines. Then, the average price stays lower as the stock rises because the same $100 *buys fewer shares*. The double line—Gain/Loss—shows a deep loss in month 13, but the effects of dollar-cost averaging (DCA) show a whopping 40% gain overall at the end of two years!

Fine. Can we stick to it? Should we stick to it?

Over 50 years ago, Benjamin Graham observed this very problem. When asked if dollar-cost averaging could ensure long-term success, Graham answered, "Such a policy will pay off eventually, regardless of when it is begun, *provided* that it is adhered to conscientiously and courageously under all intervening conditions." "Intervening conditions" are the stock market panics (Wicked Witch) and manias (Emerald City) we see the longer we invest. The prepared mind "adheres conscientiously"—stays the course—no matter what happens to the market. Possible?

Graham wasn't optimistic. He said that to be conscientious and courageous, the DCA investor must "be a different sort of person from the rest of us . . . not subject to the alternations of exhilarations and deep gloom that have accompanied the gyrations of the stock market for generations past."

Can the investor be that different sort of person? Graham said, "This I greatly doubt."

But Graham lived in a world very different than ours. Today, the majority of Americans do invest in mutual funds through employer retirement plans using DCA and do stick to it. DCA is a great way to build a wet snowball of money and watch it grow as it rolls down the hill of life—*if* you have a prepared mind.

> *The Dollar-Cost Averaging investor must "be a different sort of person from the rest of us . . . not subject to the alternations of exhilarations and deep gloom that have accompanied the gyrations of the stock market for generations past."*
> *—Benjamin Graham*

Did you know...
A lifetime of dollar-cost averaging means that each periodic purchase has less of an effect on the average purchase price (the basis) over time, just as each penny you add to a jar is a smaller percentage of all pennies in the jar. Also, at retirement and a rollover from an employer retirement plan, you are no longer dollar-cost averaging and in effect picking a time in the market to reinvest your funds. Chapter 2's The Glide Path addresses this problem and provides a possible solution through a strategy of carefully selected real estate investment trusts and closed-end bond funds.

DON'T LET THE ANCHOR SINK YOU

Nowadays everyone knows the price of everything and the value of nothing.
—OSCAR WILDE

Another way to prepare our minds is to throw off the anchor! Investors cling to the price they paid for a stock as if it were a life preserver, keeping them barely afloat while they await the safety of "getting back to even." Little do they know that this thinking is an anchor pulling them down. "Anchoring" is (yet) another bias to conquer.

People by and large believe that consistency is a sign of strength and perseverance. Whether we take a position quietly, among friends, or in public, we commit ourselves *to being right.* This is also true of any financial decision. Prospect theory research tells us that we obtain far more pain from selling at a loss than pleasure from gains, so we do anything to avoid selling at a loss, even if that money is better put to use elsewhere. We can't bear to be wrong or look bad, or worse to have to tell our partner! The price we pay for a stock is a measure of whether we are right or not, whether we are experiencing a drawdown (temporary) or a serious loss (if we sell). We have to "get back to even" to be right and not lose.

> **Did you know...**
> Prospect theory was born in 1979 and developed in a famous paper in 1992 by Nobel Laureate Daniel Kahneman and Amos Tversky. Along with Richard Thaler, the two are responsible for the behavioral finance revolution. Behavioral finance includes all the biases mentioned in this chapter and has turned the accepted economic theory of the "rational man" upside down.

Anchoring is super common. If it weren't, we wouldn't have to fight it. Buffett says, "Should you find yourself in a chronically leaking boat, energy devoted to changing vessels is likely to be more productive than energy devoted to patching leaks." The key is "chronically"—but how do we know? By throwing off the anchor to a *price*, and clinging instead to *value* as our life preserver. Then we know whether to hang on to the stock or sell it.

When we buy stock we buy ownership, however small, in a business. We should think like a buyer of the business, who wants to pay as low a value as possible and then sell, if ever, at a high value. So "getting back to even" has nothing to do with sound investing.

> **Did you know...**
> Investors confuse the stock price with the company's value. Two stocks with the *same price* can represent ownership in companies with *entirely different values*. Chapter 4 shows how to think about value, not price.

Anchoring investors simply do not know the value of what they own. Is Tom's Tomatoes down due to overall market conditions—a large tumble in the market indexes (not "chronically leaking")? Or are customers not buying Tom's red beauties because they have switched to a new variety (seriously leaking)? Have other stocks gone on sale, providing far better upside for the risk than does Tom's (change to a better vessel)? Or is Tom's in fact now such a great deal that it makes sense to buy more, not wait to "get even" and sell? These are just some of the questions that guide buying and selling. What's most important to remember is that investors who anchor to stock price, not company value, have no idea when to buy or when to sell. They are truly "at sea."

The entirely rational person treats every dollar as if it has no history, the same way a poker player says, "The cards have no memory." Treat each dollar—each hand—anew. Therefore, each dollar should be placed where it can earn the most, *no matter where it is now.* If any of the questions about Tom's Tomatoes counsels a better place for the dollar, that is where it should go. Anchoring to our buy price is the opposite of this process. It's clinging to a "chronically leaking boat" instead of "changing vessels."

Of course, if you evaluated everything you owned every day for opportunity cost, you might buy and sell like a trader! So it's important to watch the businesses you own *over time*—is the boat chronically leaking or going through normal and inevitable business and stock price fluctuations? Only by knowing the value of a business can we know how serious the leak is and whether to change boats.

Don't anchor to price; you may sink. But to know whether to hang on or swim in the direction of the greatest value, sail on to the very next chapter.

CHAPTER 4

Grading Stocks from A+ to F

To invest successfully over a lifetime does not require a stratospheric IQ, unusual business insights, or inside information. What's needed is a sound intellectual framework for making decisions and the ability to keep emotions from corroding that framework.

—BENJAMIN GRAHAM

THE SIX TESTS

Between calculated risk and reckless decision-making lies the dividing line between profit and loss.

—CHARLES DUHIGG, *author and Pulitzer Prize winning reporter*

Your attitude about stocks and management should be this: "Viewer discretion advised." For good reason. Most stocks underperform the averages. Most management teams are mediocre. Business is cutthroat, so capitalism has winners and losers. To decrease the risk of a blow up and increase the odds of picking the winners, every investment candidate must go through six tests. Think of them as subjects you took in school. Depending on how well the company's doing in a subject, it earns a grade from A+ to F. All six on the report card add up to a final grade. A stock does not have to earn all As to graduate, but it must have a B or higher average.

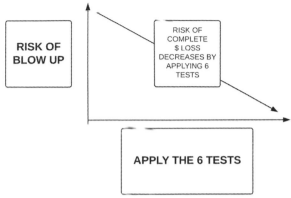

FIGURE 4.1

The six tests are:

#1 Revenue Recognition, or "mud flows downhill." If the revenue for a company is bogus or even a bit misleading, it all flows downhill like an avalanche, destroying the company's entire financial performance in its path. We want to steer clear of management teams that make sales—and customer demand--look better than they are. Earnings are questionable if revenues are suspect.

#2 Cash Flow Quality. Cash is king! A company can't spend earnings, but only cold hard (or digital) cash flowing into the company's bank accounts. Because the last and most important subject in school, shareholder yield (see below), *requires* consistent, sustainable and high quality cash flows, it's crucial to measure a stock's cash flow performance each quarter. You want real money, not management's smoke and mirrors.

#3 Earnings Quality. All the six tests contain an element of earnings quality, but this subject grades only on earnings quality factors and only on those not covered elsewhere. For example, is the management team understating expenses or overstating its profit margins? Are they using accounting shenanigans to pretty up the quarterly results for investors? If so, earnings quality is low, so the earnings number is useless.

#4 Expectations Analysis. Many investors—both individual and institutional—follow the Wall Street analysts' stock ratings and company earnings estimates. Street analysts operate in a herd, changing estimates of future earnings based on what's happened. Expectations analysis looks at a company's quality of earnings (Test #3) for the most recent quarter to determine whether they are high, low, or average quality. Then, it examines the market's reaction to the quarterly results just presented. After a bad quarter—one below expectations—the analyst herd will be slow to move estimates down. The investor may then sell or bet against the stock before analysts' estimates fully reflect the bad times ahead and investors dump the stock en masse. The investor may also buy the stock for the same reason. Analysts will be slow to move estimates up after reacting to good news. If we see high earnings quality, we can buy before analysts' estimates reflect better things ahead and investors act on those estimates. We can act on good or bad earnings quality before the analyst sheep are willing to move their estimates fully up or down in response to quarterly results.

#5 Valuation. Valuation, not price, *matters*. Valuation is the process of figuring out what a business is worth to a buyer, just as anyone would if buying a McDonald's franchise, car repair shop, or a lemonade stand (or tomato grower!). This is rooted in serious financial principles and analysis. Just as real estate investors determine what to pay for rental property, there are methods to determine the value of any business from Apple to Whole Foods Market to Home Depot.

But every now and then the clever try to move the ball. Each boom or "new era" brings silly metrics other than actual cash. In the late 1990s, investors created new metrics like eyeballs and other "new paradigms" to value stocks. This isn't "wrong," it's just for speculators, not investors, and it's a great way to lose your shirt, shoes, and underwear. They are usually pushed by venture capitalists whose interest is to get the quickest and best return on their money invested in startups, so their incentive is to show every company in the best possible light. Don't buy the hype.

Instead, buy quality stocks—those with good grades on the six tests—at reasonable valuations. The method can be multiples of earnings, cash flow, book value or price-to-earnings quality, for example, and your odds of good performance will be much better than if you are sucked into the latest fad and glossy growth story. Always think like someone buying the business, because however small your purchase is of the company, you are still becoming an owner.

#6 Shareholder Yield. Everyone knows the value and pitfalls of dividends. What everyone *does not* know is that there is more than one way to get "paid" to own a stock. Dividend yield matters, but share buybacks and debt paydown provide shareholder "yields" too. In fact, with smart buybacks as a percentage of existing shares, an investor can find not only, say, a 4% dividend yield, but a 15% or more buyback yield. The company in effect pays you 19%, but most investors see only the 4% yield. The three keys to shareholder yield lead to the most important grade of the most important test in the most important subject. Does management have the ability and desire to *increase* shareholder yield— to pay you for owning the stock? Don't trust. Verify.

> *Did you know...*
> You can find the report card—the same as what we use for Apple throughout Chapters 4 and 5—for any of the largest 750 stocks using the What's Behind the Numbers? Stock Grader app? It's available in the Apple App Store. Download the app, then just enter a stock's ticker symbol to see the grades and how it ranks against all the others. The app upgrades the report card and rankings at least monthly. *Nice!*

Insisting on high grades on these six tests, you can focus on stocks that have the best chance of padding your investment account with solid returns. To help you follow these tests, this chapter uses specific company examples where companies score well or poorly on them. It also presents Apple as an example for each test, because it has a very respectable overall grade. To start off, here's the report card for Apple, from the What's Behind the Numbers? Stock Grader app. Its overall grade ranks it 114 out of the 750 largest stocks for the month, with no change in rank from the prior month:

WHAT'S BEHIND THE NUMBERS? STOCK GRADER™

FIGURE 4.2 © Tom Jacobs and John Del Vecchio

As you read about each test, you will see Apple's grade and why it received it.

Did you know...

Any business—public or private—prepares up to three financial statements to show how it's doing. In one way or another, these are familiar to any household. They are the only information an investor needs to check what comes in, what goes out, and how it's spent.

The *balance sheet* shows the value of what the company owns—cash in checking account, buildings—and what it owes (money to suppliers, short-term and long-term loans).

The *income statement*, or statement of operations, shows revenue (sales), expenses of all kinds, taxes, net income and then earnings per share. The income statement applies accounting rules to come up with what the company owes the IRS, though we can't count on it to be what the company actually files, because its tax return is legally private.

The last is the *cash flow statement*. Since a company can only save and invest *cash* from its business, *not accounting earnings*, we need to know the actual cash coming in and going out. This statement is the most important and wasn't required for public companies until the 1980s!

TEST #1: REVENUE RECOGNITION— $#%! FLOWS DOWNHILL

I sometimes say I am a "happiness optimist" but a "revenue pessimist."

——*Economist* TYLER COWEN

The first test is whether revenue is good quality or shaky. If sales are suspect, all other numbers are questionable. It all starts at the "top line" of the income statement, so everything flows down from there. The saying "the fish rots from the head" most definitely applies to company revenue quality.

So job one is to make sure that revenue is legit. Declining revenue is normal in business and not a sign of shenanigans. Whether they sell chicken wings, sneakers, aircraft carriers, or software, all companies hit bumps in the road. The economy weakens. Customers can't spend as much. Competition increases. New technology becomes obsolete. Business is messy. Things happen.

The first test is whether revenue is good quality or shaky. If sales are suspect, all other numbers are questionable. It all starts at the "top line" of the income statement, so everything flows down from there. The saying "the fish rots from the head" most definitely applies to company revenue quality.

But fast-growing companies or those with consistent growth are victims of their own success. Wall Street rewards them with better ratings and investors are more likely to buy the stocks. The slightest bump torpedoes the stock. And the big money for management at most companies comes from stock options that pay off if the stock price rises. Bumps are not good for management's welfare.

Therefore, management teams need to keep Wall Street happy and beat sell-side analyst expectations to keep the stock price on the rise. If revenue falls short, analysts usually downgrade en masse (confirmation bias at work, ignoring whether the shortfall is a nor-

To paste over the slowdown in demand for their products and please Wall Street, execs may resort to tricks to make revenue look better than it really is.

mal business fluctuation or a serious problem) and the stock price can get hammered. So, in an effort to paste over the slowdown in demand for their products and please Wall Street, execs may resort to tricks to make revenue look better than it really is.

The most common trick is called "stuffing the channel." Here, a company entices customers to buy a product now instead of next quarter or year. This boosts revenues to make the current quarter's results look better.

Why would any customer buy earlier than it needs or wants to? Maybe the company offers a discount if the customer buys today. Maybe they allow more time to pay. Maybe they throw in a few perks like extra product or Super Bowl tickets. It doesn't matter. This is the company saying to the customer, "We'll gladly let you pay less *today* for a hamburger than *next quarter*." What customer wouldn't take that?

Did you know...
Ever hear the talking financial media heads state that a company's reported earnings "beat by a penny?" That means the company's reported results were one cent per share ahead of the average of all analysts' estimates of company earnings for that quarter or year. When a company "beats by a penny," you can bet management looked under all the sofa cushions and still only found a penny of earnings to barely beat estimates. If there were high quality earnings, the beat would have been by much more than a thin red cent. Same with "missed by a penny," where management turned over every cushion and couldn't even find a penny to meet—let alone beat—estimates!

The problem for the company and its shareholders is that stuffing the channel steals revenue from the future and pulls it into the present. There aren't *more* sales, they are just earlier. Even if the company is growing, the supply of customers to stuff the channel with will run out. Then there is nothing to steal from, everyone has bought for now, and the day of reckoning is at hand. The company falls short of Wall Street analyst estimates and it's bye-bye stock.

In 2013, speculative 3D printer maker 3D Systems scored at the very bottom—worst of all!—of the report card ranking. At the time, the company generated about 30% of its growth from stocking product with resellers (3D does not sell directly but through outlets, the way that car companies—except Tesla—currently sell new cars through dealers, not directly to the buyer.) 3D recognized—reported in their revenue line of the income statement—revenue when it sold it to these resellers. But the resellers were taking their sweet time to pay. Maybe they needed the cash for longer to keep afloat, were simply seeing how far they could go because they knew that 3D was new, unprofitable and desperate for sales so the resellers had leverage, or just weren't selling enough printers.

Regardless, accounts receivable— money resellers owed to 3D but had not yet paid the company— ballooned. By June 2013, the average receivable wasn't paid for 84 days—a whopping 25% beyond 3D's normal high-60-day range and its highest for years. There is no good or bad number for receivables; it's the trend this test examines. The trends may be

> Management's most common way to game the sales number is like borrowing from a loan shark at a higher rate (give the customer a bigger discount) to pay the one you owe at a lower interest rate (the customer paying a higher price). Eventually there's not another loan shark at any price.

good (customer paying faster, cash coming in regularly) or bad (taking more days to pay, making it harder for the company to build more 3D printers). Receivables are money owed, not cash in hand. If it's taking longer to get paid, the company isn't really growing revenue at the rate the numbers show!

There are many other ways management can accelerate revenue recognition, but sometimes it's not about their intentions but rather that Wall Street is asleep. In 2011, mandatory rule changes required Juniper Networks to change how it recognized revenue. As it happened, this provided a huge boost to sales and Wall Street was clueless, seeing only rising revenues. One of the authors appeared on CNBC and, because of this one-time event and Wall Street's reaction, he said he wouldn't be surprised if Juniper "coughed up a hairball" in the next quarter or two. That's exactly what happened. Rising revenues from an accounting change are short term, but the analysts had raised their estimates. When the company didn't meet them, the stock fell 26% in just over half a year. So-called growth stocks such as Juniper, whose revenue and other numbers are growing quickly and attract investors who drive up the price, collapse when the numbers don't meet expectations. They rarely ever recover.

All this said, *none of this is illegal.* Management teams that pull these tricks aren't being fraudulent or even dishonest, but they are hiding the fact that reported earnings are not sustainable. The company may someday collect the revenue it reported, but it can't keep selling and not collecting. This test examines the *timing* of when the revenue actually hits the checking account. The longer it takes, the harder it is for the company to keep reporting growing revenues and prop up the stock price. Don't expect Wall Street to read the fine print.

So if management is aggressive on the top line, watch out below. Mud flows downhill.

STOCK GRADER: APPLE'S REVENUE RECOGNITION

WHAT'S BEHIND THE NUMBERS? STOCK GRADER™

FIGURE 4.3 © Tom Jacobs and John Del Vecchio

Did you know...

There's an app for this! You can get the actual six test grades, the overall grade, and the monthly change in rank for 750 large stocks. Just download the authors' iOS app, "What's Behind the Numbers? Stock Grader" from Apple's App Store. Enter the ticker for any of the largest companies to obtain a scorecard, as you will see for Apple in this chapter. Note: The app's grades are neither investment recommendations, individual investment advice, nor substitutes for an investor's own analysis. They are intended to help, but not replace, your decision-making process.

Apple's revenue quality is just above average. The number of days it takes customers to pay Apple has been rising since its January 2012 nadir. Revenue *quality* isn't bad, but the *trend* isn't great. Customers are taking longer to pay:

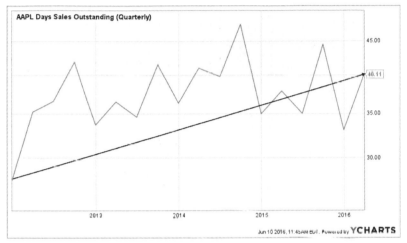

FIGURE 4.4

TEST #2: CASH FLOW QUALITY—MAMA NEEDS A NEW PAIR OF SHOES

The fact is that one of the earliest lessons I learned in business was that balance sheets and income statements are fiction, cash flow is reality.

—**CHRIS CHOCOLA**, *former President, Club for Growth*

I think that, every time you see the word EBITDA, you should substitute "bullshit" instead of earnings.

—*Berkshire Hathaway Vice-Chairman* **CHARLIE MUNGER**

"Cash is King!" You've heard that phrase a million times. In investing, it means that you cannot spend *earnings*, but only spend *cash* flowing into the company's bank account. Only if a company produces more cash than it needs to run the business can it pay sustainable dividends, buy back cheap shares or pay down debt—the three parts of shareholder yield we're after in Test #6.

> *Did you know...*
> The U.S. Securities and Exchange Commission (SEC) requires "all companies, foreign and domestic, to file registration statements, period reports, and other forms electronically"? You can find anything easily that used to take incredible effort pre-Internet. Here is the Sec.gov magic URL for company information (http://www.sec .gov/edgar/searchedgar/companysearch.html). Just enter the company name or ticker. Up pop filings.

Not surprising in a world of "viewer discretion advised," companies rarely present the crucial cash flow statement with the earnings release. So it pays to be patient and wait for this information to become available in the quarterly SEC filings. The first line item on a cash flow statement is the income statement's bottom line—net income—like the last sentence on a page that carries over to the top of the next. So, if net income has been manipulated, cash flow quality is suspect as well, *and only the cash flow statement tells the real story.* Unfortunately, because we live in a world where everyone wants everything RIGHT NOW, by the time this information becomes available—days or weeks after the earnings announcement—many investors have moved on to the next thing. Patience is the investor's edge.

The cash flow grade is based on many factors. For example, how are inventory, receivables and payables impacting financial performance? Management can manipulate these items, collectively called "working capital," to sneak a one-time cash flow boost. Can it be repeated? If not, what sly factors may have contributed to this unsustainable cash flow performance? Was cash flow propped up by acquisitions, when few acquisitions actually succeed? Because businesses have good times and bad, and because they can manipulate cash flow over the short term, the companies to own show *dependable, consistent,* and *sustainable operating and free cash flow* over time.

While a lot of factors go into our analysis, there are two rules of thumb that can simplify the approach.

> *Because businesses have good times and bad, and because they can manipulate cash flow over the short term, the companies to own show* dependable, consistent, *and* sustainable operating *and free cash flow over time.*

The first: *Decent Earnings Quality = Operating Cash Flow –*
Net Income > 0

For example, consider shares of Apple. For years, Apple has generated billions of dollars more in cash flow than earnings, in some quarters as much as $15 billion more—a lotta' iPhones. The company does not have a lot of capital tied up into its business, it turns revenue into cash at blazing speed, and it has sterling earnings quality.

The second: *"BS" Detector = EBITDA Margin TTM –*
Operating Cash Flow Margin TTM

This rule of thumb is a little more involved. It measures the relationship between Earnings Before Interest, Taxes, Depreciation, and Amortization (EBITDA) margins and Operating Cash Flow (OCF) margins. It's best to smooth this out over a trailing twelve-month period (TTM). OCF margin is what percent of every dollar of revenue the company turns into cash, which can then be used to maintain and grow the business, as well as enhance shareholder yield. The EBITDA margin is the percentage of every revenue dollar that becomes EBITDA. The company can spend EBITDA on exactly . . . nothing! In fact, Berkshire Hathaway Vice-Chairman Charlie Munger has said, "I think that, every time you see the word EBITDA, you should substitute 'bullshit' instead of earnings." Smart guy.

So: *"BS" Detector = EBITDA Margin TTM –*
Operating Cash Flow Margin TTM

There will be a spread between the two margins. Normally, the EBITDA margin is higher than the OCF margin because EBITDA excludes items that OCF includes. (The EBITDA angel cake is bigger but without more filling, because it relies on more air and lighter ingredients. A piece of OCF fudge is smaller but denser and filling, the power of each ingredient magnified.) It's not important if the spread is positive or negative. What matters is the trend of the spread. If it's widening, the company is generating more EBITDA—"BS"—than cash flow from the same dollar of sales. The company will certainly trumpet its expanding EBITDA all day long, but we should remain deaf if it's not cash money.

> *Did you know...*
> To be fair to the EBITDA cake, it has some rare and specific permissible uses, but EBITDA is *never* cash. For example, the ratio of enterprise value (EV) to EBITDA is widely and properly used to evaluate what a buyer might pay to purchase a company. If it's low enough, shareholders have some downside protection because any buyout might be at a bigger ratio. The key is that investors shouldn't invest where management trumpets allegedly good EBITDA to cover up bad trends in earnings or cash.

Triumph Group, a manufacturer of engine components (not classic sporty cars), shows the BS detector at work. Its numbers warned when Triumph's spread between EBITDA and OCF margins widened over several quarters from 2% to 3% and then to a huge 11%

for the third quarter of 2015. Because the Street follows EBITDA, the stock popped on that earnings report. But the worsening spread was the writing on the wall. When management reported sub-par results for the following quarter, the stock fell about 50%.

Tracking these two formulas shows whether a company's cash flow deserves a closer look.

STOCK GRADER: APPLE'S CASH FLOW QUALITY

WHAT'S BEHIND THE NUMBERS? STOCK GRADER™ App Store

FIGURE 4.5 © Tom Jacobs and John Del Vecchio

Apple's cash flow stands at the head of the class. It turns high percentages of revenues into cold, hard cash—and at a far higher rate than into reported earnings per share. Plus, the company mints way more cash than it needs to maintain and grow its business. That's free cash flow it can pay back to investors, which makes any company a prime candidate to pass Test #6, the "final exam" detailed in Chapter 5.

TEST #3: EARNINGS QUALITY—LEVERS ON A ONE-ARMED BANDIT

Any jerk can have short-term earnings. You squeeze, squeeze, squeeze, and the company sinks five years later.

——*Former General Electric CEO* **JACK WELCH**

Even though revenue is the essence of a company, both Wall Street and Main Street investors focus mostly on its earnings. Wall Street reports focus on analysts' consensus earnings estimates and then the financial news media obsess about every penny difference between the estimates and the results—"miss by a penny" or "beat by a penny."

However, a focus on earnings is misguided. It's earnings *quality* that matters. On a company's income statement, also statement of operations, revenue is at the top—"top line"—and earnings are at the bottom—"bottom line". The phrase "the bottom line" elsewhere means final and authoritative, but company earnings are almost always a made up number. Over 90% of companies adjust their earnings to some degree.

How can they do that? To start, accounting principles are not concrete. They can be vague or give management a lot of leeway to estimate a number here or there. There's a pretty big gap between GAAP (Generally Accepted Accounting Principles) and cash reality.

Not all of these little adjustments are important alone, but they can add up as we travel from the top line to the bottom. Let's look at this example of the different metrics on an income statement and their levels of importance:

. . . accounting principles are not concrete. They can be vague or give management a lot of leeway to estimate a number here or there. There's a pretty big gap between GAAP (Generally Accepted Accounting Principles) and cash reality.

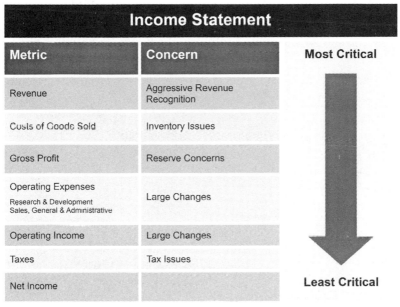

FIGURE 4.6 © John Del Vecchio

Our concerns about any of these items vary according to where it shows up on the income statement. Since revenue is at the top, that is number one. As you move down the income statement, there are various line items that impact the bottom line. For example, a company might manipulate its gross margin by writing off obsolete inventory in one quarter only to sell it at a later date and get a 100% margin boost. Cisco Systems wrote down the value of much of its inventory of telecom networking equipment when the dot.com boom ended in 2000 and choked off sales. But the company was able to sell some product eventually and the reversal looked like an uptick in growth. It wasn't.

Wall Street and Main Street get all hot and bothered by expanding profit margins. But what if those margins are an accounting mirage? What's to be excited about *then*? Don't expect anyone to do *real* work to confirm whether expanding margins are the result of better pricing of raw materials (shaky because that might change tomorrow) or increased demand (good because more customers want the company's products). People just glance at the headlines and move on.

A company could also take a bunch of charges related to the winding down of a business and create larger than necessary reserves to pay severance for laying off workers. Later the company could reverse that reserve for a 100% boost to their operating margin. Sneaky. Company execs have many (many!) ways to manipulate perceptions because they know few people pay attention. And now *you* know what to pay attention to.

Once the charade is exposed, the stock comes tumbling down. Think of each trick as an olde tyme slot machine lever that management can pull hoping to generate enough earnings to top expectations. You might get lucky for a while, increasing earnings gradually with each pull, creating a desire to want more, so you keep playing. But slots are programmed to pay out less than 100% of the amount bet over time. You can't keep it up. Same with management chicanery. Eventually there's nowhere else to turn to pretty up the true business results. Management's luck will almost always run out.

We track these tricks and score companies based on how well reported earnings match the company's true and *sustainable* earnings. This helps us steer clear of companies with a big shoe about to drop.

SOURCE: Conde Nast Collection, New Yorker Cartoon, by Leo Cullum

STOCK GRADER: APPLE'S EARNINGS QUALITY

WHAT'S BEHIND THE NUMBERS? STOCK GRADER™ App Store

FIGURE 4.7 © Tom Jacobs and John Del Vecchio

Apple scores a very low grade on earnings quality, because its profit margins have been shrinking—it earns fewer cents per dollar of sales. Growing revenues can make up for that to produce the same earnings as before, but it's tough to keep it up forever. One bad grade doesn't sink a stock as an investment, but so far, Apple's average is only slightly above C.

CHECK YOUR KNOWLEDGE #6

"There are many perfectly legal ways company management can make results look better than they really are."

ALWAYS.

TEST #4: EXPECTATIONS ANALYSIS—GETTING AHEAD OF THE WALL STREET HERD

A study of stock returns from 1994–2007 concluded that analyst forecasts were the second-most influential force on price movements. Management forecasts topped the list, according to Beverly Walther, an accounting professor at Northwestern University's Kellogg School of Management who co-authored a newly released report.

—CBS MONEYWATCH

Markets change, the leaders of the markets change, and technology that drives the markets changes, but Wall Street *never changes.* The firms and their analysts are poster children for confirmation bias: sheep roaming around in a herd and ultimately slaughtered together. As an analyst, it doesn't pay to think too differently from the crowd, because it can cost you your job. Too high or too low an estimate risks making you look foolish or incompetent when the company numbers come out. In short, the nail that sticks up gets hammered down. No wonder they all crowd around each other!

> *The Wall Street firms and their analysts are poster children for confirmation bias: sheep roaming around in a herd and ultimately slaughtered together.*

> ***Did you know...***
> The expectations game has been played since the 1990s, when analysts' aggregate predictions became widely available on the Internet.

Taken as a group, their earnings estimates move toward a "consensus," even if the analysts are certain that business will improve dramatically. Let's say Wall Street analysts expect XYZ Company to earn $1.00 per share this year but it ends up earning $1.25, blowing away expectations by 25%. A "smart" analyst on the Street who saw better than $1.00 for the year didn't come out with a $1.25 earnings target at the start. She might have stuck her neck out a *tiny bit* to $1.05 while everyone else was at $1.00. Throughout the year, if the company reports its earnings and things are lookin' good, analysts may up their estimates to $1.10, and the next quarter to $1.15. Then maybe $1.20. Soon the consensus view starts to match the financial performance the company actually realizes. On the other hand, estimates may start to decline through the same process.

We want to be ahead of—not behind—rising or falling estimates. If we look closely at the financials and see something different than the herd does, we can invest before the estimates start rising or sell before they fall. Everyone else is looking in the rearview mirror, expecting the road ahead to be smooth and safe, wrapped in their confirmation bias baby blanket. Earnings quality work ignores estimates as an investment tool but benefits from them. It evaluates the overall earnings quality of a company's reported results using a measure called Price to Earnings Quality. This helps grade the quarter on earnings *quality*, not its earnings *number*.

TABLE 4.1 How Expectations Work

IF EARNINGS QUALITY IS	AND THE VALUATION RELATIVE TO QUALITY IS	AND THE MARKET REACTS	THEN WALL STREET ESTIMATES ARE LIKELY TO	MOVING THE STOCK PRICE
High	Reasonable	Favorably	Rise	Up
Low	High	Unfavorably	Fall	Down

If earnings quality is high and the valuation of the stock is reasonable in relation to the quality of earnings, then rising estimates over the next couple of quarters are likely to attract buyers and a higher stock price. If earnings quality is low and the valuation is high in relation to the poor earnings quality, estimates are likely to come down in future quarters and bring the stock price with them. Grading earnings quality helps us lay better odds on the unknown future and then buy or sell stocks *before* the consensus view matches the company's fundamentals. No one knows what the numbers will be, but the Street is almost always complacent one way or another. Expectations are another way to help us buy lower and sell higher.

STOCK GRADER: APPLE AND EXPECTATIONS

WHAT'S BEHIND THE NUMBERS? STOCK GRADER™ App Store

FIGURE 4.8 © Tom Jacobs and John Del Vecchio

For years, Apple had a history of communicating publicly to keep expectations low but then to "surprise" with higher results. Even after years of the game, the Street kept playing along, raising estimates but not enough to look too dumb if the results were fantastic or too good if, as has happened, the string of surprises ended. Today, expectations are relatively low. An investor who thinks times will improve would find Apple's grade on the expectations test quite positive.

TEST #5: VALUATION—PAYING 50 CENTS FOR A DOLLAR

For 99 issues out of 100 we could say that at some price they are cheap enough to buy and at some price they would be so dear that they would be sold.

By refusing to pay too much for an investment, you minimize the chances that your wealth will ever disappear or suddenly be destroyed.

The margin of safety is always dependent on the price paid. It will be large at one price, small at some higher price, nonexistent at some still higher price.

—BENJAMIN GRAHAM

Next to shareholder yield (Test #6 and the next chapter all by itself), valuation is the most important test. When investors get sucked into the glossy growth story surrounding a company's prospects, they often ignore a critical factor: What valuation are they paying for those prospects? If the rosy forecast is already baked into the cake, then the upside to owning the stock is limited. Why pay $1.20 for a $1.00 bowl of soup?

Every investment must have a margin of safety, an estimate of how much can be lost if everything goes poorly. Graham wrote, "[If] the price [valuation] is low enough to create a substantial margin of safety, the security thereby meets our criterion of investment." That's why we want to find situations where we are paying $0.50 for an asset worth $1.00.

People do this all the time in the real world only to ignore it when it comes to stock investing. For example, have you ever clipped coupons? Our grandparents sure did. And the savings padded their bank account. Have you ever waited until the end of the season to buy clothes? The discounts are amazing. Many people forget all of this the minute they think about buying stocks.

Plus, when stocks are on sale at bargain basement prices, the companies may look very ugly. The stock market doesn't just give away

$1.00 for $0.50 without your having to hold your nose and close your eyes. We like to see the test scores trending up. Maybe earnings quality or the other tests' grades for a company aren't perfect, but one or more scores are *improving*. Other investors don't want the company, but that's when to look for opportunities to beat the herd.

If the report card is strong or improving and the stock is cheap enough, we will buy. It doesn't need to be on the Dean's List with As in every subject. As long as it earns good grades and detention is unlikely, the stock offers very good odds of making money.

Back to 3D Systems. The stock was trading at over 10 times revenue (forget any earnings) and the company scored Fs on all six tests. While management wasn't doing anything fraudulent or illegal, earnings quality was low and expectations high. That's a toxic mix: Just about everything had to go right for the stock to climb higher. But everything didn't and the stock got spanked, falling more than 90% from its top to its early 2016 bottom.

On the flip side was video game maker Take Two Interactive. It had been a controversial stock because its business depended heavily on one hit game, Grand Theft Auto, and new versions of it. It didn't have a Plan B, so a lot of investors were bearish. Yet in June 2014, Take Two earned the top average grade of all stocks because the six tests showed a reasonable valuation and positive earnings trends. That combination led to a very enjoyable time for investors over the next 18 months. By the end of 2015, Take Two had nearly doubled.

> *Did you know...*
> According to the Guinness Book of World Records, Grand Theft Auto V broke six sales world records. It generated the highest 24-hour revenue of an entertainment product and was the fastest to gross $1 billion. Now that's a lot of stolen cars!

VALUATION EXAMPLE: HOW TO VALUE YOUR HOUSE

What we define as a bubble is any kind of debt-fueled asset inflation where the cash flow generated by the asset itself—a rental property, office building, condo [or house]—does not cover the debt incurred to buy the asset. So you depend on a greater fool, if you will, to come in and buy at a higher price.

—*Short Seller* **JAMES CHANOS**

An example that really brings valuation home to most people is . . . their home! How often do we wonder what a house is worth? All the time. How often do we consider what another housing crash would do to it? Hmmmm . . . not so much.

Most people care only about comparable prices ("comps") and the monthly payment. But like gold or a painting, a house has no intrinsic value other than wood, windows, wiring and pipes. It's worth what people say it is. However, if you were to rent it out, it would have real value based on the amount of its net rental income. It becomes an investment with income, expenses, and profit or loss.

This is the only protection there is: If the price of any income-producing asset declines, someone will buy it when the potential income—net of expenses—is great enough to justify the price. This is exactly what happened in the housing crash of 2008. Buyers ranging from individuals to large real estate investment trusts snapped up hundreds of thousands of houses from desperate sellers. To know whether they would earn a sufficient return on their investment, they used the real estate concept called capitalization or "cap" rate. If we don't ever want to be desperate sellers—who does?—we should do the same. (Note that this does not apply to unique properties such as the White House, and gazillionaires, who have no such restraints.)

Cap rate is income minus expenses, divided by sales price, expressed as a percentage. For a home that could produce $12,000 a year net of expenses, a sales price of $150,000 results in a cap rate of 8% (8%

percent of $150,000 is $12,000). This chart shows the relationship between cap rate and sales price:

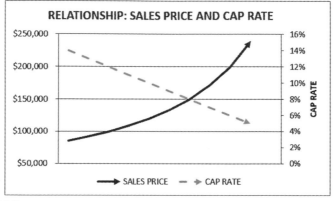

FIGURE 4.9

The chart is not dependent on the example. *For any given sales price, cap rate, or net income, the relationship between sales price and cap rate is the same.* As the cap rate (dashed line) *declines*, the implied sales price (solid line) *rises*. As the cap rate *rises*, the implied sales price *declines*. Buyers want a higher cap rate—to pay less for more. And sellers want to receive more money for less—a lower cap rate. With stocks, we want to pay a *low* multiple—such as a low free cash flow ratio, but for real estate we want a *high* cap rate—lower valuation multiple. Pay or own real estate at a high cap rate and you have a greater margin of safety. It's that easy.

But does anyone really think this way? Yes. During the boom, economist Dean Baker wrote an article explaining why he sold his Washington, DC home and became a renter. He used data showing that over time house prices are closely correlated to rental income. Certainly they may get out of whack and for a long time—just as stock valuations do—but in the end they revert to the average. Baker applied real estate finance to a situation that "felt" crazy, found he was far too exposed to wealth-destroying downside risk, and made a rational choice. He didn't *time*; he *valued*.

For such an important asset, why take the unnecessary risk of catastrophic loss that devastated people starting in 2007, from which many have not recovered? It's easy to nose around the area to estimate rental demand and potential income as if we had to rent our house. Deduct expenses and apply a rough cap rate range, say 8% to 12%. Compare the results to the price paid, what was owed and what you would need to clear if it had to be sold in a pinch—even if there is no intention to ever sell. The higher the results, the greater the margin of safety, the more peace of mind. Which is a good thing.

VALUATION: DETERMINES FUTURE RETURNS

Price is what you pay, value is what you get.

——WARREN BUFFETT

The valuation of any investment is, and always must be, a function of the price you pay for it.

——BENJAMIN GRAHAM

Future stock returns are determined by what valuation you pay for the stock. Period. Pay too high a valuation, and you immediately lower your potential returns. Pay a low one, and sometimes downside risk is so small that your upside is practically *free*.

Say you have $10 and lose 50%, leaving you with $5. How much must you gain to have $10 again? Many people understandably answer "50%," but the answer is actually "100%." Quite a difference. The smaller the loss, the lower

> *Future stock returns are determined by what valuation you pay for the stock. Period. Pay too high a valuation, and you immediately lower your potential returns. Pay a low one, and sometimes downside risk is so small that your upside is practically* free.

the hurdle. But the deeper the loss, the more it takes the Jolly Green Giant to clear the hurdle:

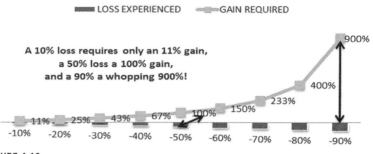

FIGURE 4.10

Not too bad at smaller losses. Stock markets as a whole present these at regular intervals and, so far, they recover. But individual stocks can do far worse and lose money permanently. Losses such as 70%, 80% and 90% require high hurdle gains of 233%, 400% and 900%. Hard to find. Consider these newer companies offering more promise than performance:

COMPANY	INDUSTRY	HIGHEST	2/4/2016	% LOSS	% HURDLE
GROUPON	Social Media	$ 31.14	$ 2.45	-92.1%	1171%
SODASTREAM	Beverage Maker	$ 79.64	$ 13.21	-83.4%	503%
YELP	Social Media	$ 97.25	$ 18.10	-81.4%	437%
TWITTER	Social Media	$ 74.73	$ 15.72	-79.0%	375%
PANDORA	Online Radio	$ 40.44	$ 8.57	-78.8%	372%
FITBIT	Wearable Fitness Devices	$ 51.64	$ 15.73	-69.5%	228%
LINKEDIN	Social Media	$ 274.19	$ 108.38	-60.5%	153%

FIGURE 4.11 Source: YCharts

Ouch. This flashes the danger of paying too much for a stock. "Too much" means value, not price. Many people who snapped up Las Vegas homes willy-nilly in the housing boom forked over way beyond any real values. It was a mania followed by a crash. Often, it's the same with stocks. Hey, *everyone* will tweet, listen to Pandora, wear a Fitbit, use Groupons, drive a Tesla or make soda at home! *It's a sure thing.* Or . . . maybe not.

Buying individual stocks requires studying the businesses and financials. Investors should know enough about the company and its valuation to buy *to* hold (open to changing views in response to new information and business progress over time), not to buy *and* hold (buy and forget). There are no stocks to hold forever. No one in the 1970s believed that Bethlehem Steel, Eastman Kodak, Woolworth's or General Motors would be bankrupt, or that currently oil and gas companies would be dying left and right. But they did and are.

If we don't know the *value* of what we're buying, how can we know if we're paying too much? And if we don't know the value of what we own, how do we know whether to sell or hold on? Lacking valuation, we become fools, gambling that a greater fool will throw more money at us. That may work, until it doesn't.

If we don't know the value of what we're buying, we don't know if we're paying too much, and we certainly don't know whether to sell or hold on.

VALUATION: TO VALUE, THINK LIKE A BUYER

Investment is most intelligent when it is most businesslike.

Although there are good and bad companies, there is no such thing as a good stock; there are only good stock prices, which come and go.

—BENJAMIN GRAHAM

When first learning about the stock market, a new investor naturally focuses on stock price. A share of Apple sells for $115, AT&T

$33, Google $667, and Pandora Radio $21. A normal first reaction is that Google must be expensive and Pandora cheap. But that's not the case.

The stock price reflects how the *market*—daily investor "auctioning" or buying and selling—values the stock. The stock's market cap (market capitalization or market value) is the number of shares issued times stock price, as with these four familiar companies:

TABLE 4.2 Stock Price By Itself Is Meaningless

MARKET VALUES	APPLE	AT&T	GOOGLE*	PANDORA RADIO
Stock Price	$100	$33	$650	$21
Shares	5.5 billion	6.15 billion	634 million	212 million
Approx. Market Capitalization	$550 billion	$200 billion	$412 billion	$4 billion

*This table averages the prices of Google's two classes of stock and combines the shares outstanding. Sept. 2015.
SOURCE: YCharts

Google's stock *price* is over five times Apple's, yet its *market cap* is only two-thirds of the iEverything company's. Pandora's price is two-thirds of AT&T's, but its market cap is one-fiftieth!

Stock price? Be gone with thee!

With stock price unceremoniously dispatched, we switch to thinking of a company *as a business we are buying*. A buyer examines all sorts of business factors and considers the value of the *enterprise*— the business—not the market cap. Market cap tells nothing about cash and debt, which are crucial to business health. All else equal, a business with more debt is less desirable than one with more cash, yet market cap recognizes neither.

Consider two tomato growers, our favorite Tom's Tomatoes and a competitor, Teresa's Tomatoes, with theoretically identical businesses, market caps, and stock prices. But Tom's company is burdened by debt needed to build new greenhouses. Teresa's managed to reach the same level of sales without debt and has put aside a nice cash pile for unknown needs. Everything equal, and knowing only these facts, would any of us pay the same to buy Tom's stock as we would Teresa's? No. Tom's enterprise is costlier to a buyer, because that buyer takes on the obligation to pay the debt. Teresa's is less costly, because of its cash and no debt. Buyers consider these when making offers. Yet the stock market assigns Tom's and Teresa's the same market cap, although they have different enterprise values.

Enterprise value is market cap plus debt minus cash. Here is an example of two similar companies with the same stock price yet with different enterprise values and different market caps:

TABLE 4.3 Same Stock Prices, But Different Market Caps and Enterprise Values

MARKET VERSUS ENTERPRISE VALUE	DELTA AIRLINES	UNITED CONTINENTAL
Same stock price	$43	$44
Delta's market cap is twice United's	$33 billion	$15 billion
United's debt is 30% higher than Delta's	+$9 billion	+$11 billion
And United has 33% more cash than Delta	-$3 billion	-$4 billion
= Delta's ENTERPRISE VALUE is 70% higher than United's, though they have almost the same stock price	$39 billion	$22 billion
Valuation requires looking at the components of enterprise value, not just the market cap that the stock market reflects. *Price (market cap) is not value.*		

SOURCE: YCharts, numbers rounded.

This is one of many ways to think like a buyer. Remember Tom's Tomatoes and Teresa's Tomatoes.

STOCK GRADER: APPLE'S VALUATION

WHAT'S BEHIND THE NUMBERS? STOCK GRADER™

FIGURE 4.12 © Tom Jacobs and John Del Vecchio

Apple scores a much-deserved A- for valuation, selling at less than 10 times price to free cash flow (anything 10 or under for a consistently cash gushing company is desirable and rare). Also, its enterprise value is 6.7 times EBITDA, in the range where a buyer might try to purchase the company. However, with an enterprise value over $550 billion, Apple is too big to swallow, but you can take a bite. Think like a buyer and take advantage of the low valuation. Anytime you can buy even a neutral free cash flow company selling for 7 or under enterprise value to EBITDA, it's as much of a softball as you'll ever see. Price (market cap) to operating and free cash flow and enterprise value to EBITDA are easy to find online, such as at Yahoo! Finance.

Now, on to the sixth and final test. It's the most important of the six for a potential stock investment to pass to give investors the best chance for profits.

CHECK YOUR KNOWLEDGE #7

"If a company is really good, it doesn't matter what you pay for its stock."

NEVER. *A company may be good but its stock valuation very expensive. Paying that price leaves too little downside protection. A company may not be as good but its stock very cheaply valued, leaving very little downside. No company is a buy at any price, but almost any company is a buy at some price.*

CHAPTER 5

The Final Exam: Putting Shareholders First

Show me the money!

—VARIOUS

TEST #6: SHAREHOLDER YIELD

Growth investors avoid companies that pay dividends and buy back stock, believing their best days are over. Quite the opposite for value investors. The best days for management moon-shot risks and fat-cat paydays may be gone, but the sweet and lower-risk paydays for shareholders have just begun.

—TOM JACOBS

The final exam tests whether the company puts us first, and it's all about what it does with the cash—*our* cash, because we as investors are the owners. You saw that Test #2 requires high cash flow quality. If it's high, management has five choices how to spend the money. All day long CEOs decide whether the put the money *here* or *there*. Their daily lives are all about opportunity cost. We want them to make choices that offer the greatest odds of success:

TABLE 5.1 5 Ways Management Spends Excess Cash and What They Mean For
Investors

WAYS TO SPEND EXCESS CASH NOT NEEDED TO RUN THE BUSINESS	ODDS OF SUCCESS FOR SHAREHOLDERS	WHY?	TYPE OF INVESTING
1) Buy property, plant, equipment (capital expenditures, or capex), beyond what's needed for business today ("growth capex")	Low	Opportunity cost is a guess	Growth
2) Enter into mergers and acquisitions	Low	Most fail	Growth
3) Pay dividends	High	Bird in hand	Shareholder Yield (value)
4) Buy back the company's own stock	Medium	Good if management buys company stock at a discount, but bad if it buys at too high a valuation	Shareholder yield (value)
5) Pay down debt	High	Reduces interest payments, pretty hard to do badly	Shareholder yield (value)

The first items are elements of "growth" investing. Companies build more manufacturing and distribution facilities, hire more software developers, buy other companies and grow empires! More often than not, these fail to create a more valuable company. The investments don't earn a sufficient return, and according to a Harvard study, roughly 85% of mergers and acquisitions fail to add shareholder value—i.e. create the conditions that increase the stock price based on fundamentals, not dreams. Think mergers and acquisitions such as AOL and Time Warner, HP and Autonomy (and many other HP acquisitions), Google and Motorola's hardware operation, Microsoft and—everything! "Growth" investing usually means less opportunity and more cost.

Simply put, most CEOs concentrate on growth investing—the first two ways to spend the cash—and don't spend shareholder cash well. How do we find the ones that do?

We test companies to see if they put us first through shareholder yield: sustainable dividends, share repurchases (buybacks) at value prices, and higher-interest debt paydown. The first pays us in cash, but the next two "pay" us behind the scenes. The more of these three ways the company pays us to own its stock, the more uncertainty is taken out of the investment decision, and the better odds of stock gains.

Beware, however. It's not enough to check the three off a list. Any management can offer shareholder yield, but few can do it *well*. Here are the good and bad ways to do it:

TABLE 5.2 Dividends, Buybacks, and Debt Reduction: Good or Bad?

GOOD OR BAD?	DIVIDENDS	BUYBACKS	DEBT REDUCTION
Good	Can maintain and even grow them	Actually reduce shares, done at cheap valuation	Pay down any debt that makes it hard for a company to survive a credit crunch
Bad	Pays too high a percentage of available cash (payout ratio), risking a dividend cut	Mask option grants so the share count doesn't decline	Pay down low interest debt, producing little savings

Applying these criteria, we restrain the CEO:

FIGURE 5.1

Did you know...
The corporate form allows people to invest in a business while "hiring" professional managers to operate the business and create value. Shareholders own the company, and the sole job of management is to increase the value of their investment.

Management and shareholders often disagree on:

- what creates value,

- whether to focus on short-term or long-term profits,

- the welfare of employees versus cost cutting, and

- what risks to take to grow the company.

And, of course, how much management should receive in salary, stock options, and perks!

Today, shareholders of public companies have no real power unless they own a huge percentage of total company shares. The best thing investors can do is simply avoid or sell stock in companies that do not treat shareholders well—those that do not provide shareholder yield.

Shareholder yield removes cash from management's hot little hands. It limits their choices so they don't blow our money on skittles and beer. Paying down debt saves on interest payments, freeing up more cash. If the company's shares are selling at a price that places a very low value on the company, buying its own stock is a good investment. And when the company buys back shares, our shares own more of the company, earnings and cash flow per share increase, and the stock price eventually rises.

Plus, if a company pays dividends, every share it buys back eliminates paying the dividend on that share, *forever*. If the dividend yield is 4% a share, the company "earns" 4% a year forever just by not paying it out to that share anymore. The Rule of 72 and doubling periods tell us how powerful a cash creator this is—and the extra cash is available to increase the dividends, buybacks, and debt paydowns. It's a virtuous cycle:

FIGURE 5.2 © 2016 Thistle Associates

The investment strategy therefore is: (mostly) small cap stocks + cheap valuation (Test #5) + free cash flow (Test #2) + one or more of sustainable dividends, buybacks at a discount, or paying down higher interest debt. Despite this simple thinking, most growth investors avoid companies that pay dividends and buy back stock, believing their best days are over. Quite the opposite for value investors.

BAD SHAREHOLDER YIELD

There are many . . . ways that a CEO can hurt a company, but they all boil down to a CEO putting his or her own interests before the company's. With the mystique surrounding the superstar CEOs, it is easy to forget that their job is to serve the company and its shareholders, not pad their own wallets.

—**ANDREW BEATTIE,** *Investopedia*

Management is not all evil, but the system provides bad incentives. There are two major problems.

Problem #1 is that a large part of management's wealth is tied to the performance of the stock. They may have stock options or restricted stock units, or cash awards related to the performance of the stock price. The better the stock does, the more they make. In some ways, this is a good thing. We want management teams to be motivated and share in the wealth creation. But, problem #2 often conflicts with this goal.

Problem #2 is that the lifespan of a CEO at a corporation has declined from 10 years to about 5½ years since the 1990s. So the incentive is to make the money and run. Because the big payday is from stock options, management has to keep ahead of analyst estimates quarter after quarter. When business is not running all that smoothly, they know the clock is ticking to come up with creative ways to please Wall Street. Management will do anything to meet Wall Street earnings expectations—even though they know they will run out of accounting ammunition at some point—because by then they probably will have collected their loot, skedaddled, and left the mess for the next CEO. The system's incentives make this very rational behavior.

> A CEO may only be around five or 10 years. The incentive is to make the money and run.

> *Did you know...*
> The average CEO tenure has decreased from about
> 10 years to about 5½ years since the 1990s—Challenger,
> Gray & Christmas (USA Today).
>
> Nearly 40% of CEOs are fired within their first 18 months
> on the job—Center for Creative Leadership (Peter Barron
> Stark).
>
> The average tenure of a departing S&P 500 CEO in the
> U.S. is 8 years as of 2010, down from 10 years in 2000—
> Conference Board report (WSJ blogs).
>
> In 2012, 15% of the world's largest 2,500 companies
> replaced their CEOs—the second-highest figure in the
> 13 years it {Booz Allen} has compiled the data. (In 2011,
> 14% of this class of executives were replaced.)—(The
> Daily Beast). *See Booz & Co. 2012 Chief Executive Study.*
>
> **SOURCE:** http://theamericanceo.com/2013/07/22/new-forbes
> -post-no-country-for-new-ceos/

No wonder some management teams try to make shareholder yield look great while the business around them is imploding. They may take on debt in order to buy back stock. That might not be bad if the company's growth prospects are fantastic and the return on their capital is higher than the cost of funding those projects (a leveraged recapitalization, or "levcap"). This is so difficult to do successfully, however, that few try. (You'll see one of those rare and beautiful jewels, AutoZone, later in this chapter.)

What if the business is in a death spiral though? Propping up the earnings per share by buying back stock wastes the cash lifeline. There used to be a big title insurance company, LandAmerica, which would insure titles for many of the houses bought in the U.S. (you likely know the familiar "Chicago Title," another title insurance company). In the housing crisis, the company kept buying back boatloads of stock as it fell 100% and into bankruptcy. This wasn't sound investing of shareholder money; it was reckless destruction. Management must have seen disaster unfolding, but they didn't know what to do. "Don't just do something, stand there" would have made more sense. Keeping the cash cushion may or may not have prevented bankruptcy, but spending it left only one outcome.

Or a company uses too much high interest debt to fund the dividend when cash flow evaporates. It doesn't want to lose all the investors who own the company because of the quarterly check. At the hint of a dividend cut, shareholders run for the exits, which kills the stock price.

At the hint of a dividend cut, shareholders run for the exits, which kills the stock price.

The plummeting stock angers Wall Street analysts who then lower their estimates. The board of directors pressures the key executives who start to feel the heat. CEOs step down. Class action law firms file suit. It's an ugly cycle, and investors lose.

So, just because a company pays a high dividend or buys back an Everest of stock doesn't mean it's a good thing. What matters is that the business is in fine enough shape that dividends and buybacks are the *best* uses of cash. Anything less is "bad" shareholder yield. Let's go through the three shareholder yield elements part by part—test by test.

DIVIDENDS—THE GOOD AND THE BAD

Beware stocks that pay outsized dividends in comparison with their peers. Often, when a company's share price suffers, they cut dividends, which hurts the share price more.

—**TED SCHWARTZ,** *ABC News*

Dividend analysis for shareholder yield is crucial. Fortunately, it's brief and easy. Does the company have enough cash on hand and coming in to maintain the current dividend through thick and thin, and potentially grow it? This is not difficult to answer.

The guideline is that a company should not pay out more than 50% of its net income or free cash flow in dividends. No matter how good their quality, enough earnings or cash flow must be available for the inevitable rough patches a business goes through. An investor does not want to own a stock yielding 4% only to see it cut when the company needs cash, because investors will sell en masse and the stock losses will dwarf any dividends received. Who wants a 4% dividend when the stock drops 30%? We require a company to have a cash cushion so that it doesn't have to cut the dividend to make one.

> *The guideline is that a company should not pay out more than 50% of its net income or free cash flow in dividends.*

Be very suspicious. Too often investors are suckered by a high dividend, but it isn't solid. Here's what usually happens.

Did you know...

It's often said that dividends provide a majority of the stock market's returns. But this ignores the fact that dividends have been taxed at widely different rates at different times. Dividends' contributions to returns are significant, but it's not so simple.

Bad Dividend Case Study: CenturyLink

TABLE 5.3 Good and Bad Dividends

GOOD OR BAD?	DIVIDENDS	BUYBACKS	DEBT REDUCTION
Good	Can maintain and even grow them	Actually reduce shares, done at cheap valuation	Pay down any debt that makes it hard for a company to survive a credit crunch
Bad	Pays too high a percentage of available cash (payout ratio), risking a dividend cut	Mask option grants so the share count doesn't decline	Pay down low interest debt, producing little savings

CenturyLink provides local exchange, long distance, and broadband access in 37 states, but most of its revenue comes from its huge but declining plain old telephone service, called "POTS" in the industry.

CenturyLink has been a high yielding stock. However, in late 2012 the whopping 7.5% dividend yield was in danger of being cut. If management slices a large dividend, investors sell and it's the guillotine for the stock. In a desperate and unsustainable way, CenturyLink puffed up earnings until the day of reckoning.

Starting at the top line—revenue—the company said it was counting lease income as revenue. This was a policy at one of its acquisitions, Qwest, but no one was buying its new parent CenturyLink's stock for money it earned from leasing out old-school phone lines. The reason to own CenturyLink and competitors Windstream, and Frontier Communications was for the big dividend, with *maybe* some growth in providing Internet service to balance the decrease in landlines and the steady cash the traditional phone business produced.

So if CenturyLink could show *any* revenue growth, no matter how small, and maintain the dividend, it could counter the stereotype of being a rusty old landline company, hold on to shareholders, and keep the stock price up. But without counting lease income as revenue there would be nothing to show against the declining POTS revenues. No one knew how big a part leasing was of sales, but it was certainly important enough to require CenturyLink to disclose the item in its SEC filings—where few look, but where all the bodies are buried.

The company also changed the way it calculated its customer base, making growth look better than it was. CenturyLink counted an access line when service *started*, not when the customer *actually paid* first and subsequent bills. That's like selling someone a product and not getting money in any form—cash *or* credit—to pay for it and saying you *were paid*!

Did you know...
A company must reserve an amount on its balance sheet for estimated future pension obligations—"pension liabilities"—to its retired employees. To keep the number down and show better (but not real) financial health, companies often model a high return for what they will earn every year on money set aside for pensions. This is perfectly legal. However, when the investment profits come in less than the estimate, the true financial picture emerges, and the stock usually gets slammed. States like Illinois and California, as well as local governments, face the same pension problem and are unable to raise taxes enough to fix it.

The company also played with the depreciation and amortization expense—what they were able to deduct because the accounting world's rules on the useful life of its lines gave them bigger deductions and more earnings. (Companies are allowed to deduct the cost of their landline networks over time—depreciate them—from their income, which reduces their taxable income and taxes they have to pay.) This is also true for rental and other commercial real estate.

But at some point you can only depreciate the property to zero and poof!—no more benefit. Not only that, but CenturyLink, like many others, used unrealistic assumptions on how well their investments would cover pensions, and you can't keep that up forever either.

By excluding certain items beginning in June 2011, CenturyLink could boost "adjusted" EPS the next three quarters by more than 70% compared to what the old method would have produced. This had nothing to do with the strength of its business but everything to do with accounting sleight-of-hand. All of this should scare away anyone from wanting to own a poor scoring stock despite its juicy yield, no matter how seductive it is in a low-interest world.

But there was yet another and subtler red flag. CenturyLink used a capital lease to help fund its property, plant and equipment purchases in 2011. Think of a capital lease simply as debt, and you can only take on so much. In the several years prior to 2011, the company had not used any capital leases but suddenly added $700 million. This looked like cash generated by the business, and it did indeed pay for capital expenditures, but it was a one time thing. It was clear that a capital lease could not be used again. To keep afloat, the company would have to slice the dividend.

And that's what happened. CenturyLink cut its dividend and the stock got hammered. No one knew when it would happen, but close attention to numbers showed that it eventually would. The only people who can tell you when something will happen are liars. But anytime a debt-laden company pays a very high dividend—no rule, but certainly over 10%—consider this suspicious. You don't have to read the fine print. Just don't let greed over the dividend prevent you from balancing the income from the dividend against whether it's worth the hit the stock would take from a cut.

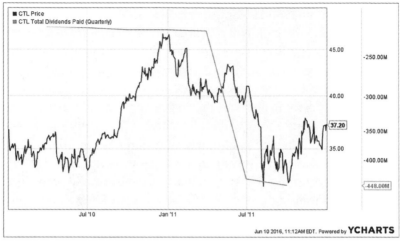

FIGURE 5.3

Basically, if a dividend seems too good to be true, it almost always is.

STOCK GRADER: APPLE'S SHAREHOLDER YIELD—DIVIDEND

Apple's dividend is both good and true and yields 2.3% of the stock price today. The company stopped paying a dividend in 1995 and resumed in late 2012. From that point, the chart shows the stair step in cash dividends paid per quarter (lower line), while the payout ratio (top line) is steady and even declining since mid-2013, currently paying a low 24% rate (as a guideline anything under 50% is great):

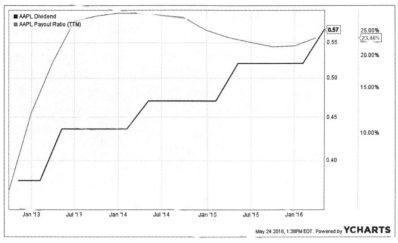

FIGURE 5.4

This leaves a humongous upside to increase the dividend at a steady clip, as it has done every year since restarting the dividend (the stair step line). It also puts the risk of a deadly dividend cut as close to zero as you can get.

CHECK YOUR KNOWLEDGE #8

"A lower dividend can be better than a higher one if the company is less likely to cut it."

ALWAYS. *A secure 3% beats a 9% dividend that, when cut, will cause the stock to drop substantially.*

BUYBACKS—THE GOOD AND THE BAD

There is only one combination of facts that makes it advisable for a company to repurchase its shares: First, the company has available funds—cash plus sensible borrowing capacity—beyond the near-term needs of the business and, second, finds its stock selling in the market below its intrinsic value, conservatively calculated.

—WARREN BUFFETT

The sound finance rule is that every management decision to spend money has to be where it can earn the most return. Sometimes it's right to buy the company's own stock.

To understand buybacks, think of stock as money—a currency. If you create it—sell new shares adding to your share count—you create more shares but reduce ("dilute") the value of the currency, just as when the Federal Reserve increases the money supply. Doing that too much can lead to inflation, which is another way of saying that the value of money—its purchasing power—is reduced. Companies can use their stock the same way as currency. When everyone wants to buy it, the company can sell shares at a high price to raise money. When no one wants to buy, it can buy its own shares at a sale price. This is the smart use of money we prize in management.

Good management is in the best position to know whether the stock is undervalued. Emotion kicks stock prices to the curb all the time. If a company's own stock is selling for a good discount, it not only makes sense to buy it, it should probably be required. In theory, you could then sell more shares at a higher price later, but what you have done is increase the value of the remaining shares, the opposite of what happens if you issue shares.

> *If a company's own stock is selling for a good discount, it not only makes sense to buy it, it should probably be required.*

TABLE 5.4 Good and Bad Buybacks

GOOD OR BAD?	DIVIDENDS	BUYBACKS	DEBT REDUCTION
Good	Can maintain and even grow them	Actually reduce shares, done at cheap valuation	Pay down any debt that makes it hard for a company to survive a credit crunch
Bad	Pays too high a percentage of available cash (payout ratio), risking a dividend cut	Mask option grants so the share count doesn't decline	Pay down low interest debt, producing little savings

Every sound buyback *must* look something like this, which is the gold standard:

We believe the current price of our stock to be at a significant discount relative to the value of our assets and our dividend payments," said Dave Schulte, [CorEnergy Infrastructure Trust] President and Chief Executive Officer. "As we continue to assess which uses of capital would be most accretive to our shareholders in the long term, we believe repurchasing shares to be an attractive investment opportunity."

Succinctly, "Our shares are cheap relative to true value, and they are a better use of your cash than other opportunities." Yes, it's a press release, and yes management will show itself off to best purpose, but it's pretty hard to falsify the value and shareholder yield mindset you see here. CorEnergy was selling for a fraction of the value of its hard assets, pipelines, storage facilities and more. But because oil prices had crashed, every stock with "energy" in its name plummeted. Not to buy back shares would have been just plain dumb and definitely the wrong way to treat investors.

Perhaps not surprisingly, buybacks may be a sleight of hand. Many companies, primarily those that issue a lot of stock options and happen to reside in a certain valley of tech innovation in the Golden State, will buy back shares because they fear that if shareholders knew how many options were issued—how many new shares were being added—they would not like it.

This practice takes *our* money—because we own part of the company—and buys back shares, so that when the company issues options to employees, the share count doesn't rise. The company actually uses our money to buy shares at *higher* prices so they can reissue them as options at *lower* prices. The options then show up in the diluted share count, but who's squinting to see? They shrink the value of our ownership and use our own money to do it!

Unbelievably, though fortunately, some companies are so unwitting that they actually admit the buybacks are to compensate for option grants and insult us directly:

> *Under the new stock repurchase program, which is designed to return value to Adobe's stockholders and minimize dilution from stock issuances . . .*

The argument about "tech" company options is always that "We have to do it in our industry because we couldn't hire any software engineers if we didn't." That may be true; we are not Silicon Valley HR managers. *But you don't have to own the company's stock.*

So as not to pick on Adobe, here's the far more egregious Ford:

> *Ford Motor Company announced today that its board of directors has approved a repurchase program for up to approximately 116 million shares of Ford common stock, which will offset share dilution and help improve shareholder returns.*

There are seven—yes, seven!—references in the same Ford press release to the need to counter dilution. (Think of the emperor riding through town bellowing, "I'm not wearing any pants!") Unbelievable that people accept this. Sure, it would "help improve shareholder returns," if shareholders weren't struck dumb already by dilution from stock option grants.

At least we can faintly praise Adobe and Ford for being upfront. The more common press release says nothing, really, and makes you wonder what they've got up their sleeve:

> *The stock buyback plan reaffirms our confidence in the company's strategy and long-term growth potential. It also demonstrates our ongoing commitment to delivering value to our shareowners," said Frederick W. Smith, chairman, president and chief executive officer of FedEx Corp. "Our strong balance sheet provides us with the flexibility to initiate this stock repurchase program while continuing to execute our strategic growth initiatives.*

This is like saying, "Well, we have all this cash and don't know what to do with it, so we guess we'll buy back some stock." Such analysis! Mr. Smith has too many titles. No one is challenging him to think clearly. He should learn the number one lesson: Companies should buy back stock *only* when it is the best use of shareholder money. That's only when the stock is on sale and better than other investment alternatives. Period.

> **Did you know...**
> Buybacks are a relatively new practice for companies.
> They were in effect banned in the U.S. until the 1980s,
> out of concern management would use them to
> manipulate share prices. Rules loosened after the Carter
> Administration began to deregulate many industries,
> a trend which sped up in the Reagan years. For tax
> reasons, some investors prefer them to dividends. A
> company is taxed on its net income, from which it pays
> out any dividend. Then, the dividend recipient—the
> shareholder—pays taxes on dividends received (though
> there is no tax on dividends paid into tax-advantaged
> accounts in the year paid). A company is not taxed on
> share repurchases.

Bad Buyback Case Study: IBM

There used to be a saying that "you can't get fired for buying IBM"
products. (Talk about confirmation bias.) Recently, it's been more
accurate to say that investment managers should get fired for buying
IBM *stock*. Ol' Big Blue ain't what it used to be.

Initial concerns about IBM were entirely qualitative, not quantita-
tive—not about the numbers. It faced increased competition when
big contracts came up for renewal. In the old days, those renewals
were almost certain to be awarded to IBM, often with *no* competition. But the market dynamics had changed and no one could be certain of anything, except that competition means you have to lower
your prices to both snare and keep business.

About those numbers.

Revenue growth was slowing and went negative 4% year-over-year in late 2014. Then sales really collapsed with double-digit declines over the next several quarters. Business was getting worse and worse. Analysts' estimates couldn't come down fast enough and the company regularly fell short of *substantially reduced* revenue expectations by another $500 million to $1 billion! This was a company taking in $81 billion a year, sure, but with sales dropping already, another several percentage point drop is deadly. All the Street cares about are the reported numbers versus analyst expectations. And these shortfalls pressured management to do something to avoid Wall Street's hatchet.

Meanwhile receivables started to tick up each and every quarter. This suggested the company might be stuffing the channel and borrowing from future revenues by offering customers extended payment terms. But if you pull a customer's purchase from the June quarter into March you have to replace that purchase with one from another customer the next quarter to offset the future revenue loss. It's like borrowing from a loan shark at a higher rate to pay off the current one. And because IBM's business was getting worse, not better, there was no way out: cement overshoes lay ahead. If IBM failed to deliver on earnings expectations or—gasp!—cut its dividend, the stock would be toast. So management took on a bunch of debt in order to buy back stock and make sure the dividend was safe. *We're talking adding billions of dollars in debt to pay investors.*

Debt per share exploded by over 40%. Cash flow stagnated. Meanwhile, buybacks lowered the share count often by 5% or more *each quarter*. This boosted EPS (earnings per share) because net income was divided by fewer shares, but at some point buybacks can't save EPS if revenues decline enough. Eventually investors caught on and sold off the stock. From a high of $216 in 2014 IBM fell to $118 in early 2016, a decline of 45%. During most of that decline, U.S. stock indexes were hitting new highs.

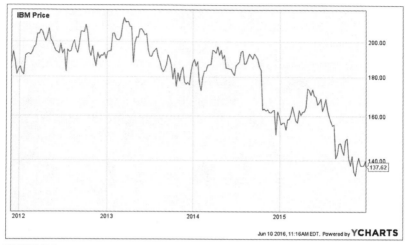

FIGURE 5.6

Maybe if Wall Street weren't ruled by short-termism, IBM's management would have had more leeway to turn the business around. Debt could have been used to finance an acquisition in a higher growth sector that really could have moved the needle (though most acquisitions are duds for shareholders). Management could have redirected the business toward higher return projects—if the same team that couldn't do it before somehow got the magic touch. The table at the beginning of this chapter showed that both of these are riskier "growth" ways to spend company money, but IBM used bad buybacks and dividends in a hopeless attempt to paint over the rust. But rust never sleeps. It always wins.

For buybacks and dividends to work, a business has to at the very least have steady free cash flow or better. Remember, there is no "must have" stock, despite the money the financial "services" industry spends to make us think there is. This is *your* money. You do not *have to* own IBM. A mother once told her daughter after a breakup that men are like buses. There's another one along every 15 minutes. Stocks too.

Bad Buyback Case Study: Hewlett Packard

Share buybacks, such as at IBM, don't work with a business in decline. Free cash flow must be at least neutral if not growing. Margins must be stable. Where there is only bad news, buybacks may boost earnings per share for a time, but no one really benefits except shareholders unloading the stock, Wall Street bankers earning fat commissions on the buyback program, or executives cashing in stock options. It ends badly.

One of the other big disasters in the mid to late 2000s was Hewlett Packard. The company was bogged down by bloated acquisitions and a series of mishaps that led to huge write-offs against earnings. Messrs. Hewlett and Packard were probably rolling over in their graves as their company spiraled out of control. *Billions of dollars* of shareholder value simply dried up, like HP printer ink in the desert.

Meanwhile, the company repurchased about $50 billion in stock from 2006 through 2011. That's the GDP of South Africa! Yet with the business sinking, buybacks couldn't prop up the stock, which by the end of 2012 was off more than 70% from its highs just a few years before.

> *Did you know...*
> In 2010, Hewlett-Packard purchased Palm, the maker
> of the early smartphone "Palm Pilot." Palm dropped the
> "Pilot" name due to a trademark infringement lawsuit by
> Pilot Pen Corporation.

Plus, management's record of buying companies was *terrible*. The Compaq acquisition worked out poorly. And Palm—how's that Palm Pilot working out today?—became a tech relic. Someone didn't do their due diligence on Autonomy either and HP paid too much for a business that wasn't what it seemed. So, investing those $50 billion in even more doomed projects wasn't the right way to go. Management clearly needed to get their hands out of the cash register. They could at minimum have spent the cash on higher dividends. The increased yield would entice an entirely new and longer-term shareholder base and put a firmer floor under the stock price.

By the end of 2012, expectations were so poor that Hewlett-Packard actually earned higher grades not only on the expectations test, but all the others. The fundamentals had simply bottomed out, the earnings quality started to improve, and the stock price was finally cheap. We know from the valuation test that almost any business is a buy at *some* price, and HP hit that mark.

Into 2013 and 2014, free cash flow actually expanded. The operating cash flow margin increased and accelerated to exceed net income by $1.2 billion to $2.6 billion *per quarter*. A percentage point here, a percentage point there, and pretty soon a company's annual numbers are up a lot. Meanwhile, receivables and inventory came back under control. As you'd expect, shareholders gained. From the end of 2012 through 2014 the stock zoomed more than 260%:

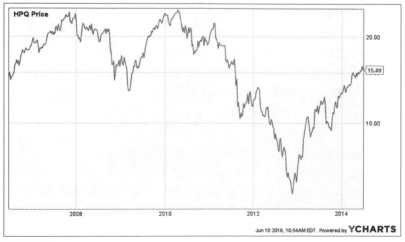

FIGURE 5.7

Too bad HP management wasted cash at higher prices buying back stock to prop up earnings per share, like LandAmerica the title company, but at least HP didn't go out of business. Even just letting the money pile up in the checking account would have been better. Desperation rarely leads to good decisions—or investor gains.

STOCK GRADER: APPLE'S SHAREHOLDER YIELD— BUYBACKS

The Big Apple scores well here. Since restarting its dividend in 2012, Apple has been a hungry buyer of its own shares, which have proven to be undervalued. The buybacks not only increase our ownership, raise earnings and boost cash per share, but also increase the cash available to hike dividends and increase buybacks—the shareholder yield virtuous cycle:

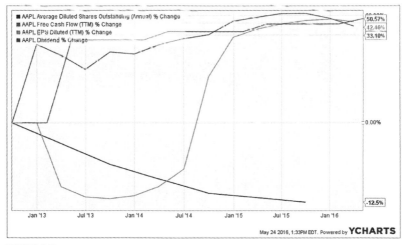

FIGURE 5.8

Note that this is a logarithmic, not linear, chart (explained in Chapter 2). As buybacks reduced shares a whopping 12.5%—one-eighth of the company—in three years, earnings and free cash flow per share vaulted, as has the dividend.

CHECK YOUR KNOWLEDGE #9

"When a company buys back its own stock, it's not creating jobs. It's a waste of money and not good for the economy."

SOMETIMES. *It might be a waste of money for the company to repurchase stock if at a high valuation. But at a low valuation, it's good for the company and the economy. In a capitalist system, we want companies to put shareholders first. If buying undervalued stock is the best thing to do with the money, that's best for everyone.*

PAYING DOWN HIGH INTEREST DEBT

There are but two ways of paying debt: Increase of industry in raising income, increase of thrift in laying out.

—THOMAS CARLYLE

Annual income twenty pounds, annual expenditure nineteen pounds nineteen and six, result happiness.

Annual income twenty pounds, annual expenditure twenty pounds nought and six, result misery.

—WILKINS MICAWBER *in Dickens'* David Copperfield

Debt paydown is easy to understand, because everyone who uses a credit card can play along. Let's say you carry a $1,000 balance at 15%. Every dollar you pay off saves you 15 cents a year in interest. That's a 15% gain, in effect, and a great return on investment. It gets even better. Credit card debt is revolving, so you pay 15% on a dollar balance *every year.* So paying off a dollar saves 15% every year *forever,* just the way buying back a share of a dividend-paying stock saves having to pay the dividend each year. Both create more cash by reducing obligations.

There are some advantages to company debt, however. A business can deduct interest from income for tax purposes, just as we can with our home mortgage interest. This can make debt very attractive for companies that plan to use it for projects that may earn them more than the cost of interest (one measure of opportunity cost). Second, company debt can be bonds, which pay out interest and then the full amount of the debt at maturity, but companies typically never pay it off, refinancing debt into the future (as homeowners often do as rates decline). However, companies can and do have revolving loans, lines of credit that are like credit cards, or a home equity line of credit, and paying those down offers the same immediate savings as when paying off credit card debt.

Good Debt Paydown Case Study: Cincinnati Bell

TABLE 5.5 Good and Bad Debt Reduction

GOOD OR BAD?	DIVIDENDS	BUYBACKS	DEBT REDUCTION
Good	Can maintain and even grow them	Actually reduce shares, done at cheap valuation	Pay down any debt that makes it hard for a company to survive a credit crunch
Bad	Pays too high a percentage of available cash (payout ratio), risking a dividend cut	Mask option grants so the share count doesn't decline	Pay down low interest debt, producing little savings

We've already seen some terrible debt situations, where IBM and Hewlett-Packard not only didn't reduce debt, but increased it for dividends, buybacks and acquisitions that *destroyed value*. So it's a pleasure to offer a success story with Cincinnati Bell.

You might think after reading about CenturyLink that telecoms are lousy businesses, but good management can work wonders. Cincinnati Bell has made smart moves to increase shareholder yield through debt paydown.

Lenders happily lend to companies with dependable cash flows because of the low risk of default. There are hardly any more dependable ones than telecoms, cable or satellite TV. The monthly income from customers is sticky; it's a hassle and often costly to change providers. Someone has to stay home from work waiting for the cable guy, for example. The catch for the children of the AT&T breakup is that they had to find some other source of stability or even growth, because their old line telephone business—once dependably throwing off cash like shoppers on Black Friday—was slowly but definitely declining. Cell phone use led customers to cut the landline cord. The companies paid high dividends because it made no sense to invest in more copper phone lines. What to do?

Cincinnati Bell promoted President Ted Torbeck to CEO on Jan. 31, 2013. The company already had the smarts to develop the cutting-edge business of providing data centers—"colocation" or back up—for businesses. Cincinnati Bell then spun it off as a separate company, CyrusOne, trading on the stock exchange by itself. The parent retained a large amount of CyrusOne shares which, as is often the case with spinoffs, were worth way more with CyrusOne as a separate company than when investors treated it as part of Cincinnati Bell. Then Torbeck did two more important things.

First, he said that the company would increase its investment in delivering phone, TV and lightning fast Internet services to homes and businesses via fiber optic networks. This is the "triple play" more and more common around the country. But, unlike most companies that invest in new lines of business, Torbeck said bluntly that if the fiber optic services didn't deliver the returns on investment the company required, it would stop putting money into them. However, the company knew its customer base. Though small relative to the behemoths like CenturyLink, Windstream and Frontier, it has a strong and loyal following in Cincinnati and that part of the state. Customers have grabbed the chance to buy these services from the hometown company rather than from "big bad" Time Warner. It may have been growth use of capital, but the company made a very low-risk decision with very good potential upside. This was good opportunity cost thinking and it's worked out well.

Torbeck also devoted cash from CyrusOne stock to pay down debt. The company says it will continue paying down debt, grow revenues enough in fiber to offset the decline of its traditional telecom business, and become more valuable to shareholders. Here's the proof so far:

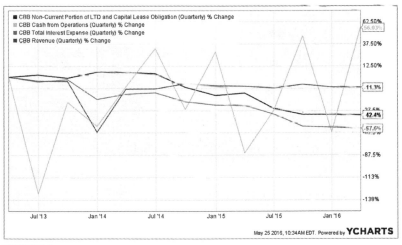

FIGURE 5.9

Since Torbeck took over as CEO on Jan. 31, 2013, revenue is off 11%, but notice that the decline stopped in the quarter ending July 2014 and revenues have stabilized for almost two years. Then, paying down 42% of long-term debt has sliced Cincinnati Bell's trailing-12-month interest expense by a huge 57%. Voilà, cash flow from operations jumps 56%. These are *astonishing* numbers over any time period, let alone only three years. This is how high interest debt paydown can work wonders, even if revenues are flat. Sooner or later, there will be cash to resume a dividend and/or buy back shares. The company will become very valuable to a buyer. These are three catalysts to the stock price that are likely to make investors very happy, and all from one element of shareholder yield.

> *Did you know...*
> Speaking of Cincinnati Bell . . . Until a 1984 court order, AT&T (and General Telephone and Telegraph, to a smaller degree), had a monopoly on "plain old telephone service" (POTS) to your home or business, as well as payphones (remember them?). You couldn't touch the wiring outside or inside or connect any other equipment than Ma Bell's. The breakup into regional companies— "Baby Bells"—was to increase innovation and competition. CenturyLink, Windstream, Cincinnati Bell, and Frontier Communications are the most well-known of the Baby Bells surviving in different forms today.

Case Study of an Exception: Debt for Brilliant Buybacks at AutoZone Leads to 3,200% Gain in 15 Years

One of the greatest value creations in investing history shows when and how debt for buybacks works wonders.

A boring business familiar to all of us vaulted 31 times—*3,200%*— over 15 years, or 28% annualized. Good luck finding that from any investment for that long! Not only that, but the company and stock weathered the 2007–09 credit crisis and Great Recession quite well, even though AutoZone loaded up on debt. Long-term investors have been well rewarded. Moreover, the method AutoZone employed has been used elsewhere and will be again. It's very rare, but this is not a one-time opportunity.

Pretty much everyone knows and has been in an AutoZone store. Each has very low opening and operating costs and benefits from efficient nationwide inventory and supply chain systems. The staff is knowledgeable and customer-oriented. Often, they'll lend you a tool or two to work on your car, right in the lot.

But it took vision to bring the really big gains. In 1999, money manager Edward S. Lampert started buying up AutoZone stock to obtain a controlling position. He influenced the company to spend its extra cash—free cash flow—to buy back shares, instead of on willy-nilly expansion.

That's heresy to retailers or chains of any type. They believe *they have no choice but to expand*. It's in their blood. Yet eventually the heedless expansion stories end poorly. There are fewer untapped markets and each additional store is less profitable than the last. Still, many retailers over-expand, compete with themselves, face ruinous competition, fail to change, and fade or blow up. Boston Chicken, Einstein's Bagels, Circuit City, Linens N Things, A&P, Radio Shack, Blockbuster, Borders, Sbarro, Friedman's, Brookstone, Quicksilver, Eddie Bauer, Wet Seal, and American Apparel all filed for bankruptcy at one point.

Lampert's idea was *not* to expand or die. He believed simply, if you have a decent business, why not take the cash you don't need to run it—the free cash flow—and, instead of blowing it on ruinous expansion, invest it to build value for shareholders? (Shocking, right?) If a company's shares are cheap, either because of emotional selling, poor overall market conditions, or just plain ignorance of a business's virtues, those shares are a better investment than yet more stores for expansion's sake, offering weaker and weaker results. And sometimes though shares may look expensive today, if you are a Lampert you can estimate the upside to your strategy with reasonable accuracy.

If execs do this correctly, the number of shares drops. If shareholders sit tight, doing nothing, suddenly whatever they own is a larger percentage of the company than before. Consider a company's stock to be a pizza. You own one of ten slices. The company buys back one slice, reducing slices from 10 to nine. You owned 10% of the company, but now you own 11%. Then, the company buys back another slice, and you own 12.5%. So? If you spread a company's net income (or free cash flow) across fewer shares, it goes up! Spread $10 across ten shares, and that's $1 a share. Spread it across 8 shares, and EPS becomes $1.25. If the valuation remains the same at 10 times earnings, the stock would rise from $10 to $12.50, a 25% gain while you do nothing at all. And if earnings rise? Better gains.

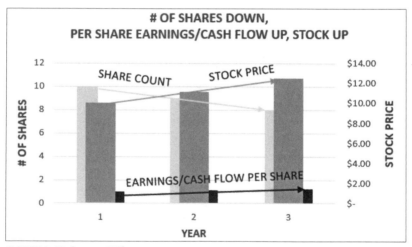

FIGURE 5.10 Source: YCharts

This is what happened at AutoZone. Management took extra cash—cash not needed to keep stores going or open new stores—and instead of burning it up at the track or through ruinous expansion, used the cash and low-cost debt to buy back 78% (yes, you read right—almost 80% of the company) of its shares. Where did the debt come from? Because the company employs its low-cost efficient model in smaller towns and niches where it is less likely to face competition, it produces dependable cash. Lenders love a low-risk borrower, so they compete to lend by offering lower rates.

Here's how it's worked, from around the time Lampert gained control to today. Management continued its practice after Lampert's 2013 exit for investor benefit:

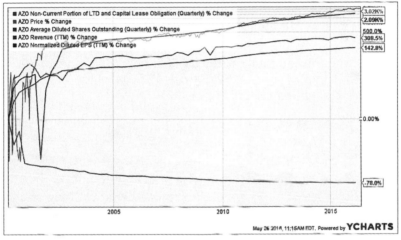

FIGURE 5.11

It's impossible to emphasize enough each element of the AutoZone success story:

- Buybacks reduced the share count by an unheard of 78% . . . fueled by debt that grew 308% (four times).
- And while revenue grew a mere 142% (1.5 times) and net margins only doubled . . . the effect of the buybacks boosted EPS 2,090% (21 times)!
- With an average P/E ratio of 16 over the entire 16-year period . . . *the stock price vaulted 3,200% (an astronomical 31 times), an annualized return of 28%!*

Meanwhile, the company expanded margins, squeezing just a few more pennies out of every sale, and fueling a stock already on fire. *But even without that—even if the profit margins had remained the same*—stock gains would still have been astounding.

Massive debt-fueled buybacks transfer company profits from selling shareholders to fewer remaining ones. It's powerful but poorly understood. Some value investors—and few others—watch for these "leveraged recapitalizations" ("levcaps" to the cool kids, which readers are), such as AutoZone.

Armed with this information, the investor naturally responds:

- How do I know *before?*
- When do I buy?
- When do I sell?

This is not as hard as it seems. In this case, Lampert drove the process. This is his M.O. He's done it successfully at clothing retailer The Gap, car dealership chain AutoNation, and discounter Big Lots (and less successfully at Sears Holdings, though with all the spinoffs of Sears companies such as Land's End, Seritage Growth Properties REIT, and Sears Hometown and Outlet Stores, this story is far from over). Follow Lampert. Create a Google News alert that sends you emails about Lampert. Watch where he's gaining control. Buy when he does and sell if he does. It won't work every time, but his record has been pretty good.

Did you know...
It's not hard to follow the moves of a company, such as share repurchases, or important investors such as Lampert and master levcap media mogul John Malone. Set a Google News alert for your keywords and you will receive email alerts at whatever frequency you want.

Setting Up a Google Alert:

1. Go to google.com/alerts

2. Enter what you want alerts for. Google will show you how many or few matching items will show up in alerts. You create alerts for one content area at a time.

3. If you are happy with the results, click "Create Alert." Otherwise, edit your content description until you are satisfied.

4. After you "Create Alert," you will see your new alert term at the top of your list. Click the pencil icon to the right to choose among many options, including how often you want alerts, how many items you want to receive, and your delivery address.

Voilà! Sit back and wait for the information to come to you, and enjoy becoming well-informed about anything you want!

There you have it. This is a very rare instance where debt for buybacks is permissible and profitable. While AutoZone stock likely does not offer this magnitude of returns ahead, for over 15 years, long-term investors were truly in the zone with AutoZone.

STOCK GRADER: APPLE'S SHAREHOLDER YIELD— DEBT PAYDOWN

Apple is in an interesting position. Like many multinationals, it has gobs of cash overseas, which, if repatriated to the U.S., would incur tax. To avoid that bite, Apple borrows cheaply in the U.S. to buy back shares. This is very different from the AutoZone story; Apple's 12.5% buyback in three years doesn't touch AutoZone's, but the principle remains. If you can borrow at a rate that's cheap enough so that it's worth buying your even cheaper stock, you do it all day long.

Apple has debt, but it's so low interest there's no need to pay it down. The company doesn't, and that's good.

Now, how does Apple score on shareholder yield, the sixth and most important test? Putting together its dividends, buybacks and debt, Apple earns a fine B+. Across all the tests, Apple scores extremely well. With an overall grade of A–, it ranks 114 out of 750 large companies.

WHAT'S BEHIND THE NUMBERS? STOCK GRADER™

FIGURE 5.5 © Tom Jacobs and John Del Vecchio

CLOSING

Before you place your financial future in the hands of an adviser, it's imperative that you find someone who not only makes you comfortable but whose honesty is beyond reproach.

—BENJAMIN GRAHAM

Most people are not do-it-yourself investors and prefer to work with a financial or investment advisor. Keep in mind that these are different people. A financial advisor is compensated by commissions on sales of products, such as mutual funds, variable annuities, or whole life insurance policies. That advisor is also subject to a loose standard called "suitability," where the advisor's only obligation is to choose or recommend investments that are "suitable" for the client. This standard, vague enough to allow most anything, has allowed advisors to make money *off* of clients, rather than *for* them, because it allows them to put their own interests ahead of their clients'! Though an annuity of any kind, whole life insurance, and mutual funds with "loads"—initial commissions—are not right for just about everyone, apparently they are "suitable" for many.

The investment advisor, on the other hand, has a fiduciary responsibility—to put *your needs first*. You would think this true of a financial advisor, but now you know it's not. The investment advisor earns a percentage of your account balance, so the incentive is to grow it. This does not make the advisor a good manager, but it's the right incentive structure.

> **Did you know...**
> The government has recently issued new regulations
> that will apply the stricter fiduciary standard to financial
> advisors, but not in all circumstances and not until 2017.

There are two things to keep in mind. First, if any advisor, of any kind, keeps you from blowing up money in poor investments, that's good. Seriously. The opportunity costs of the fees charged, as you know from the Rule of 72, can compound substantially over time, but if your advisor helps you sleep at night and your account growing over time, that's probably more important to you. Just make sure to review your statements and ask about every investment and product the financial advisor sells or tries to sell you.

The investment advisor can charge too much, too. Anyone who charges more than 1% of assets per year had better be worth it, and few are. It's routine to walk into a big name office such as Merrill Lynch or Wells Fargo and find yourself paying 1.5%, 2.0% or worse! That's a pretty high hurdle for "better be very good." Why put up with that? One percent per year should be the max, and the more money you have, the more the fee should drop from there.

The benchmark is always the Vanguard Group, a non-profit family of inexpensive mutual funds that follow indexes. It was founded by the legendary John "Jack" Bogle. Bogle is justly famous because he showed that actively managed—and usually high commission—mutual funds' performance didn't justify the fees. Vanguard is about passive investing—there is no active manager behind the scenes pulling the management strings—and charging the lowest possible fees. In fact, some firms that offer index funds charge 1% or higher, while the Vanguard 500 Index Trust index fund charges . . . 0.16% a year.

> *Did you know...*
> If you believe you have been treated unfairly or
> unethically by your advisor, you may file a complaint with
> the Financial Industry Regulatory Authority (FINRA),
> finra.org. FINRA handles thousands of complaints each
> year and also conducts mediation and arbitration.

But this begs the question. How do you know, other than by fees, what you are getting, whether from Vanguard or Merrill Lynch or another contact who is a financial or investment advisor? By now, you know everything you need to ask, ask, ask and keep asking until you get good answers, not things that sound good but are empty calories. Find out exactly how any financial person is paid, exactly what service you should expect, and what every investment means and why it's in your account. Know that an investment advisor is less likely to advise you on household finances, insurance and other planning, while a financial advisor is going to be less knowledgeable about the nuts and bolts of your mutual funds or stocks.

CHECK YOUR KNOWLEDGE #10

"If fees consume more than 1% of your assets annually, you should probably shop for another adviser."

ALWAYS. Benjamin Graham, *The Intelligent Investor*

Think of yourself as a patient going to a doctor or a client to a lawyer. Many of us find these difficult situations in which to be assertive. Healthcare today leaves little time for doctor-patient interaction, and even though younger doctors are far less imperious than ones trained decades ago, the setting gives the doctor a certain psychological power. True for the lawyer, as well, though you usually receive a free consultation, after which the billable hours ramp up. You must ask about everything, get second opinions, and take control.

This is exactly the same need with any financial professional. *Be assertive.* You may enjoy anything to do with money management as much as eating sawdust, but why would you treat your money with any less care than your health or legal problems? It's like anything you do for the first time, no matter how hard. It gets easier with practice. If you get pushback or sales pitches or something that seems fishy to you, it probably is. Scram.

This book is designed to help you to gain confidence and ask the right questions. Few people you will ever meet will understand shareholder yield, but the principle of putting shareholders first applies across the board, whether in stocks or mutual funds. If your advisor can't explain how a stock or fund is good to investors, keep asking until you get it put clearly and simply. Now, some advisors love their work and research so much that they may want to talk your ear off, but the best will sum it up without blather first. The worst will show their ignorance quickly, not even able to parrot the firm's canned research or marketing materials from mutual fund companies.

Just watch out for sales over substance. There's a reason salespeople who are good . . . are good! They know how to make it personal—develop a relationship based on golf or clubs or whatever—without the chops to back it up. They know exactly what to say at any point to keep you on board, and they know that once they snare you, it's hard for you to break off the relationship. No one likes to do that.

You can choose a better advisor following Fox Business's Maurie Backman's guidance that a good advisor:

• Talks openly about risk
• Makes sure you understand what fees you are paying

- Tries to educate you about investing
- Asks to meet regularly to review your portfolio
- Remembers your goals (and cares about them)

And if you are going to manage your own investments, you should be well-equipped now to decide what suits your personality and goals. The Rule of 72 has presented a framework for finding companies that put shareholders first. The Apple app—*What's Behind the Numbers?* Stock Grader—is a helpful tool to help you check up monthly on the stocks you already own (though not as a recommendation to buy or sell).

In the end, the beginning of this book is still the most important thing: The Rule of 72. Your money is wet snow rolling down a long hill. Use the Rule to weigh every financial decision's opportunity cost, the impact of earning and spending, and to keep focused. The financial world is a conspiracy to keep us from patience, questions, and common sense. If you hear, read or see information that is designed to make money matters sound complex and the presenter oh-so-very intelligent, *rebel*. Money and investing should be no more complex than a simple rule about how to double your money. Ben Franklin knew it centuries ago and proved that it works.

Be like Ben.

An investment in knowledge pays the best interest —BENJAMIN FRANKLIN

BIBLIOGRAPHY

Del Vecchio, John, and Jacobs, Tom, *What's Behind the Numbers? A Guide to Exposing Financial Chicanery and Avoiding Huge Losses in Your Portfolio* (McGraw-Hill, 2012) (see Chapter 6)

Faber, Mebane, *Shareholder Yield: A Better Approach to Dividend Investing* (Mebane Faber, 2013)

Fraser, Steve, *Everyman A Speculator: A History of Wall Street in American Life* (Harper Perennial, 2006)

Graham, Benjamin, *The Intelligent Investor, Revised Edition* (Collins Business Essentials, 2006)

Graham, Benjamin, *The Memoirs of the Dean of Wall Street* (McGraw-Hill, 1996)

Greenblatt, Joel, *You Can Be a Stock Market Genius: Uncover the Secret Hiding Places of Stock Market Profits* (Fireside, 1997)

Juglar, Clément, *A Brief History of Panics in the United States* (Cosimo Classics, 2005)

Kindleberger, Charles, *Manias, Panics and Crashes: A History of Financial Crises* (Wiley, 2005, 5th edition)

Madrian, Brigitte C., and Shea, Dennis F., "The Power of Suggestion: Inertia in 401(k) Participation and Savings Behavior", NBER Working Paper No. 7682, Issued in May 2000

Mandelbrot, Benoit, and Hudson, Richard L., *The Misbehavior of Markets: A Fractal View of Financial Turbulence* (Basic Books, 2007)

Munger, Charles, *Poor Charlie's Almanack: The Wit and Wisdom of Charles T. Munger* (The Donning Company, 2005, Expanded Second Edition), edited by Peter D. Kaufman

Peris, Daniel, *The Strategic Dividend Investor* (McGraw-Hill, 2011)

Priest, William W., and McClelland, Lindsay H., *Free Cash Flow and Shareholder Yield* (Wiley, 2007)

Spier, Guy, *The Education of a Value Investor* (Palgrave Macmillan,

2014)

Swenson, David F., *Unconventional Success: A Fundamental Approach to Personal Investment* (Free Press, 2005)

Taleb, Nassim Nicholas, *The Black Swan: The Impact of the Highly Improbable* (Random House, 2010).

Taleb, Nassim Nicholas, *Fooled by Randomness: The Hidden Role of Change in Life and in the Markets* (Random House, 2008)

Thaler, Richard, "Mental Accounting Matters, Journal of Behavioral Decision Making," J. Behav. Dec. Making, 12: 183–206 (1999) http://faculty.chicagobooth.edu/richard.thaler/research/pdf/MentalAccounting.pdf

Thorndike, Jr., William N., *The Outsiders: Eight Unconventional CEOs and Their Radically Rational Blueprint for Success* (Harvard Business Review Press, 2012)

Tweedy Browne, "What Works in Investing, Studies of Investment Approaches and Characteristics Associated with Exceptional Returns," http://www.tweedy.com/resources/library_docs/papers/WhatHasWorkedFundOct14Web.pdf

EQUATIONS

Chapter 1:

72 / Annual Rate You Project = Number of Years It Takes to Double Your Money

Years in Which You Want Your Money to Double / 72 = Annual Rate Required

Real Return = Your Gain – Inflation

Nominal Return = Your Gain

Chapter 4:

Market Capitalization = A Company's Diluted Shares Outstanding × Stock Price

Enterprise Value = Market Capitalization + Debt – Cash

Chapter 4, Test #2:

Decent Earnings Quality = Operating Cash Flow – Net Income > 0

"BS" Detector = EBITDA Margin TTM – Operating Cash Flow Margin TTM

EBITDA = Revenue – Expenses (excluding interest, taxes, depreciation and amortization)

Chapter 5:

This book's preferred investment process =

(Mostly) Small Cap Stocks + Cheap Valuation (Test #5) + Free Cash Flow (Test #2) + One or More of Sustainable Dividends, Buybacks Below Fair Value, or Higher Interest Debt Paydown.

GLOSSARY TERMS

Ask: The price a stock seller will accept to sell shares higher than the Bid.

Bear Market: A 20% or more fall from a market index's last peak.

Behavioral Finance: An economic field that studies irrational psychological and behavioral variables involved in investing in the stock market.

Benchmark: A standard, used for comparison. For example, the NASDAQ may be used as a benchmark against which the performance of a technology stock is compared.

Bid: The price a stock buyer offers to pay a seller lower than the Ask.

Bonds: A company borrows money by issuing bonds. Bond buyers are lending money to the company in exchange for payments of interest and principle. (Think of this as the Bank of You.) Most people never own individual bonds, instead choosing simplicity and diversification through bond mutual funds or ETFs (exchange-traded funds), which are mutual funds you can buy and sell like stocks throughout the day, rather than mutual funds which only trade once a day after market close.

Broad-Based Index: An index whose purpose is to reveal the performance of the market, such as the S&P 500 or Wilshire 5000.

Bull Market: A rise of 20% or more from a market index's last trough.

Buying on Margin: A risky technique involving the purchase of securities with borrowed money, using the shares themselves as collateral. Usually done using a margin account at a brokerage, and subject to fairly strict SEC regulations.

Capitalization or "Cap" Rate: The discount rate used to determine the present value of a stream of future earnings. Equals normalized earnings after taxes divided by present value, expressed as a percentage. See housing valuation example in Chapter 4.

CDs: Certificates of deposit. Banks pay interest to customers who lock up their money—agree not to withdraw it—for a period of time. The interest is higher than in a savings account because of the lockup.

Compound Interest: Not only does your money earn an interest rate, but also as time passes, it earns interest on the interest. This creates a snowball effect. In fact, it grows *exponentially*—the snowball that blanketed Chicago!

Consumer Price Index (CPI): An inflationary indicator that measures the change in the cost of a fixed basket of products and services, including housing, electricity, food, and transportation. The CPI is published monthly. It is widely used but seriously flawed.

Deflation: A declining price environment, which increases the purchasing power of money. Think the falling cost of computers over the last decades. Widespread deflation is bad for the economy, because people don't spend. They know they can purchase more for the same money tomorrow. See Japan for the last three decades.

Depression: A decline in real GDP of 10% or more, or a recession lasting more than 2 years.

Dividend: A taxable payment declared by a company's board of directors and given to its shareholders out of the company's current or retained earnings, usually quarterly. Dividends are usually given as cash (cash dividend), but they can also take the form of stock (stock dividend) or other property.

Dividend Yield: The yield a company pays out to its shareholders in the form of dividends. It is calculated by taking the amount of dividends paid per share over the course of a year and dividing by the stock's price.

Dollar-Cost Averaging: An investment strategy designed to reduce volatility in which securities are purchased in fixed dollar amounts at regular intervals, regardless of what direction the market is moving. Thus, as prices of securities rise, fewer units are bought, and as prices fall, more units are bought. This reduces the volatility of the purchase price.

Drawdown: Decline in value of an account from peak to trough.

Earnings Before Interest, Taxes, Depreciation, and Amortization (EBITDA): An approximate measure of a company's operating cash flow based on data from the company's income statement. Calculated by looking at earnings before the deduction of interest expenses, taxes, depreciation, and amortization. Widely used but flawed in most cases.

EDGAR: Electronic Data Gathering, Analysis, and Retrieval. The SEC's system used by all public companies to transmit required filings, such as quarterly reports and annual reports and ongoing disclosure obligations. You can find the filings at sec.gov.

Enterprise Value: A measure of what the market believes a company's ongoing operations are worth. Enterprise value is equal to a company's market capitalization − cash and cash equivalents + preferred stock + debt.

Equity: Ownership interest in a corporation in the form of common stock.

FOMO: "Fear of missing out," today's lingo for the fear of choosing to spend time *here* when you could be missing out on something better *there*. This illustrates opportunity cost.

Generally Accepted Accounting Principles (GAAP): A widely accepted set of rules, conventions, standards, and procedures for reporting financial information, as established by the Financial Accounting Standards Board. Leaves room for management judgment.

Government-Backed Securities: Specifically, bonds or bills issued by the U.S. Treasury and backed by the "full faith and credit" of the

U.S. Unless the government defaults, the owner is certain of being paid interest and principle. Believed to be safest non-physical asset investment in the world.

Gross Margin: Reveals how much a company earns taking into consideration the costs that it incurs for producing its products and/or services. It is equal to gross income divided by net sales, and is expressed as a percentage.

Inflation: A rising price environment, which reduces the purchasing power of money. If inflation is high, it encourages people to spend now, rather than later, when their money will buy less.

Liquid Asset: A type of asset that can easily be converted into cash.

Margin: Using money borrowed from a broker/dealer to purchase securities; the amount of equity required for an investment in securities purchased on credit; the face value of a loan minus the value of the pledged collateral.

Margin Call: A call from a broker to a customer (called a maintenance margin call) or from a clearinghouse to a clearing member (called a variation margin call) demanding the deposit of cash or marginable securities to satisfy the Regulation T requirements and the house maintenance requirement for the purchase or short sale of securities or to cover an adverse price movement. Usually not good for the customer.

Market Cycle: Periodic up-down, high-low movements that happen in all markets; any price that goes up must come down too. Looks like a sine wave. In stock markets, a market cycle is said to be complete when the Standard & Poor's composite index (S&P 500) is 15 percent above the lowest point or 15 percent below the highest point. The stock market cycle is a leading indicator of the business cycle, and mirrors changing investor sentiments.

Mental Accounting: Mental accounting occurs when investors mentally compartmentalize assets such as stocks, bonds, real estate or accounts. A key concept in behavioral finance.

Mutual Fund: An open-end fund operated by an investment company which raises money from shareholders and invests in a group of assets, in accordance with a stated set of objectives. The most common investment class for individual investors.

NASDAQ: One of the two major marketplaces (exchanges) for buying and selling stocks in the U.S. It was called the "over the counter" market before "NASDAQ."

Net Income: For a business, what remains after subtracting all the costs (namely cost of business, depreciation, interest, and taxes) from a company's revenues.

New York Stock Exchange: The other of the two major forums for buying and selling stocks in the U.S.

Nominal and Real Interest Rate: If you earn 5%, that's the nominal rate. But if inflation is 2%, you really only gain 3%. That's the real (inflation adjusted) rate.

Operating Cash Flow (OCF) Margin: Actual cash generated by a company's operations as a percentage of revenues.

Operating Margin: Operating income divided by revenues, expressed as a percentage.

Opportunity Cost: When you compare putting your money here or there, the "cost" is what you might have gained by taking the other course. This is easiest when making a consumer purchase. Your opportunity cost is what that could have earned if invested. Every dollar spent is not one dollar, but that dollar plus its earnings over the rest of your life.

Ponzi Scheme: A form of fraud where the perpetrator promises to take in money and pay out an alluring profit. But the perp doesn't invest it. The payout comes from more new money coming in. Eventually, not enough money comes in to pay the prior investors, and the whole thing falls apart, with those participating in the scheme losing most or all of their money.

Price/Earnings (P/E) Ratio: The most common measure, but flawed, of how expensive a stock is. The P/E ratio is equal to a stock's market capitalization divided by its after-tax earnings over a 12-month period, usually the trailing period but occasionally the current or forward period. Value investors generally do not use the P/E ratio, finding ratios of free and operating cash flow to be more reliable.

Recession: Two consecutive quarters of falling real (adjusted for inflation) gross domestic product (GDP).

Regulation T: A Federal Reserve Board regulation that governs customer cash accounts and how much credit broker or dealers may extend to customers to purchase and carry securities. See also Margin.

Relative Returns: How one investment performs relative to a benchmark. As opposed to absolute returns, which are returns relative to zero (or the rate of inflation).

Revenue Recognition: When the amount of income is recorded on the company's financial statements.

Russell 2000: The best-known of a series of market-value weighted indices published by the Frank Russell Company. The index measures the performance of the smallest 2,000 companies in the Russell 3000 Index of the 3,000 largest U.S. companies in terms of market capitalization.

Stealth Tax: If inflation is low enough, people may not notice. Their money is being "taxed"—taken away from them by inflation—but stealthily.

Stocks: When you buy stocks, you have part ownership of a business. Also known as "equities." You have equity in the business, just as if you went into business with a partner.

Valuation: The process of determining the value of an asset or company. There are many techniques for valuation, and it is often partially objective and partially subjective.

Volatility: The relative rate at which the price of a security moves up and down.

Yield: The annual rate of return on an investment, expressed as a per centage; for bonds and notes, the coupon rate divided by the market price; for securities, the annual dividends divided by the purchase price.

The above definitions were either written by the authors or came from Investor Words (www.investorwords.com).

INDEX